With a Little Help from My Friends

Born in 1951 in an army family, educated at St Stephen's College Delhi and St Catherine's College Oxford (as a Rhodes Scholar), **Dev Lahiri** worked as a tea planter, lecturer in history and an editor before switching to teaching. He began his career as a teacher/Housemaster at Doon School and then went on to head Lawrence School, Lovedale and Welham Boys' School, Dehradun. He lives with his wife, Indrani and their two dogs, Zak and Ellie, in Dehradun.

With a Little Help from My Friends

A Schoolmaster's Memoirs

DEV LAHIRI

Published by
Rupa Publications India Pvt. Ltd 2016
7/16, Ansari Road, Daryaganj
New Delhi 110002

Sales centres:
Allahabad Bengaluru Chennai
Hyderabad Jaipur Kathmandu
Kolkata Mumbai

Copyright © Dev Lahiri 2016

The views and opinions expressed in this book are the author's own and the facts are as reported by him which have been verified to the extent possible, and the publishers are not in any way liable for the same.

All rights reserved.
No part of this publication may be reproduced, transmitted, or stored in a retrieval system, in any form or by any means, electronic, mechanical, photocopying, recording or otherwise, without the prior permission of the publisher.

ISBN: 978-81-291-3788-3

Second impression 2016

10 9 8 7 6 5 4 3 2

The moral right of the author has been asserted.

Printed by Shree Maitrey Printech Pvt. Ltd., Noida

This book is sold subject to the condition that it shall not, by way of trade or otherwise, be lent, resold, hired out, or otherwise circulated, without the publisher's prior consent, in any form of binding or cover other than that in which it is published.

CONTENTS

Foreword	*vii*
Preface	*ix*
1. Childhood with the Army	1
2. The Graduate	14
3. St Stephen's—Rediscovered	22
4. The Interregnum	29
5. St Stephen's—The Second Innings	35
6. At The Crossroads	40
7. Oxford Ahoy!	44
8. The Oxford Experience	49
9. Barsati Days	66
10. The Winter of '79	69
11. Married Bliss?	71
12. The Corporate Bubble	74
13. Crossroads Again	77
14. Doon Days	81
15. Off to Lovedale	92

16. Beneath the Beauty	95
17. Into the Fray	100
18. Matters of the Heart	122
19. Trouble in Paradise	127
20. The Crisis Deepens	141
21. The Battle Continues	148
22. In the Wilderness	160
23. Oh Kolkata!	167
24. The Welham Chronicles	173
25. The Struggles	184
26. Boys Will Be Boys?	190
27. The Heart Rules the Body	197
28. An Abrupt End	204
29. The Wasatch Epilogue	214

FOREWORD

All who are engaged in teaching children in schools have an onerous responsibility of shaping a person who essentially is capable of sustaining a successful livelihood which is cocooned in uncertainties, failures, successes and progress. To teach to chart a course through an unpredictable future, to understand and accept change, to understand one's role in the community are the imponderables that become the syllabus of an educator over and above imparting the skills of the 3 R's. The overwhelming demand of the latter subsume the needs of true education that prepares for life and puts the teacher in a real dilemma.

Dev Lahiri solved this problem by using his own life experiences in his interaction with children. So be it road running, facing the most adverse personal difficulties, pursuing his interests with single minded dedication, never wavering from the values learnt from his humble middle class upbringing, he made sure that his students shared his interests, learnt his values and were as uncompromising as him in upholding truth and integrity. His totally child-centred approach singles him out as an unique teacher of young minds.

Rhodes Scholars are undoubtedly exceptional and most rise to prominence of leadership in their countries in various and diverse fields. Of all the careers that Rhodes Scholars have chosen after their education, surely school teaching must be a rare exception. Yet it is probably one of the most important professions to choose as one quietly and without fanfare, and I might say much recognition, shapes the lives of thousands of children to face the future. Equipped with his personal qualities of integrity, grit, determination and a sense of fun, this Rhodes Scholar in my mind stands out as having served the objectives of the Scholarship in its fullest sense and provided leadership in a sphere that truly builds on the foundation of a country.

I am glad that Dev has penned his experiences. They are all to do with how his life evolved from a schoolboy into a school teacher and subsequently as a Principal. There is much to read and learn from. All school teachers should understand from this important autobiography that they are indeed people who play a very important role which more often than not goes unsung.

Shomie Ranjan Das
Retd Head of Mayo College, Ajmer, Lawrence School,
Sanawar and Doon School, Dehradun

PREFACE

'Do not judge me by my successes, judge me by how many times I fell down and got back up again.'
—Nelson Mandela

This is, strictly speaking, not an autobiography. I am aware that my life is not important enough for people to spend hours poring over a book on it. Yet bits of my life have been extremely interesting; especially a few events and the people involved in them. If nothing else, I hope the reader finds some entertainment value in the pages that follow. Perhaps what could be of interest are the insights into human behaviour on issues like honesty, trust and integrity.

There have been grave injustices in my life. Yet this is not an exposé. It is, however, an attempt to put on record for the first time, my side of the story and in so doing perhaps be the voice for many Heads of Schools who may have suffered in the manner that I have. It would also provide, to those who are interested, a glimpse into the way some of our better-known institutions are run and how difficult it can sometimes be for those on the spot to deal with the powers that surround them. If I have written about specific instances and specific people who I think have been less than fair with me, it is not as an attempt to get 'my back' on them or in a spirit of rancour, but as an attempt to expose the vulnerability of people in my position.

The position of Head of School in our country, particularly in a residential school, is not an easy one. We are the chief administrators, chief security officers, chief personnel managers, chief educationists—all rolled into one. We have little or no training for the job. Moreover we have many different constituencies to answer to, be it the governing body, the parents, the faculty, the students, the support staff or the alumni. On several occasions these constituencies have conflicting interests. To add to our woes we have no union to stand up for us in times of need.

In penning the pages related to my headship of schools, I have been acutely aware of the loneliness of this position and I hope that in so doing I have been able to portray to some degree the difficult nature of this job.

Whilst I cannot dream of being in the same league as the Natwar Singhs of this world, I suppose that some at least might be interested in the travails that even ordinary mortals such as headmasters of schools have to go through. One then gets some idea of what the man-on-the-street has to endure.

When I look back, I believe my life, on the whole, has been a fairly remarkable journey. If I am still around to tell my story, it is largely because of the kindness of a large number of friends and well-wishers and that includes my own family and my old students. It is to them that I dedicate this book.

1
Childhood with the Army

My mother was seven months pregnant with me when she was bitten by a supposedly rabid dog. I am told that I was delivered almost as soon as the course of injections (fourteen in those days) was administered. This, I suspect, has a lot to do with the madness that seems to have constantly haunted my life ever since. This particular incident could also account for my love for dogs to this day.

My childhood was much like that of any other army brat; a series of postings to locations both interesting and boring. This meant that I was enrolled in a series of different schools. When I was three, my older brother, then seven, was packed off to a boarding school. Whilst this was probably a well thought out move of my parents to secure a steadier education for him, it unfortunately created a huge gap between my brother and I. I ended up going to a different boarding school a few years later. Although my brother has stood by me through thick and thin, it has only been a few years since we have managed to bridge the gap and become the best of friends.

The strongest impressions of my early childhood are those of my father. This seems rather paradoxical given the fact that he hardly ever communicated with us and was always a distant figure. But his ramrod straight appearance and his uniform, the combination resulting in his nickname, 'Lofty' had a great impact on my young mind. In addition, he set the highest standards of behaviour for us to follow. I remember distinctly, while other officers would have no hesitation in bundling their families into the official transport and taking them shopping, we always walked or took a tonga. I remember the battalion 'bania' coming to our house with a huge box of sweets on Diwali and being uncseremoniously asked to leave with the admonishment, 'You think I can't afford your bloody sweets,' ringing in his ears.

My mother too was a remarkable woman in her own way. She was a graduate in English literature from Calcutta University, (no mean feat, especially for a woman in those days) and was one of the most voracious readers I have ever known. Coming from a middle-class Bengali background, it must have been difficult for her to adapt to the demands placed on an army wife, but she coped remarkably well and entertained all my father's brother officers and their families with great aplomb.

Throughout my life in boarding school there was nothing I looked forward to more than her long handwritten newsy letters. Her penmanship was remarkable. It was devastating to see her slip into depression and then dementia in her last years. To see a person once so exuberant and fun-loving reduced to a mere shell was one of life's crueller lessons.

One particular incident made an extremely powerful impact on me and to a great extent shaped my entire outlook on life. When I was about eight years old my father was posted to Mhow, a military cantonment in the state of Madhya Pradesh. As was the custom in those days, we were allotted a bungalow with a sprawling compound. Some quarters stood adjacent to these homes inhabited by a community of families, some of whom in exchange for the use of these quarters and a little extra money, would help with the chores in the house.

To one such family belonged a little boy called Ramu who soon became my closest friend. Ramu and I would spend hours outside our respective school hours, playing. One fine day we decided to step out to a nearby maidan to play a game of cricket. We carried a bat and ball with us. In the middle of our game, there was a sudden thundershower and the heavens opened up on us. Both of us sought shelter under the nearest tree. As we were standing there, our neighbour, a certain Colonel Naidu drove past in this blue Fiat car. Seeing us, he stopped and signalled to me to hop in. Without a thought, I jumped into the car, thankful for being rescued from the pelting rain.

Colonel Naidu drove me home and left me at our front porch where my father was attending to some potted plants. Seeing me, my father asked, 'Where is Ramu? I thought he went with you to play.' I cheerfully embarked upon an explanation of how the kind Colonel had offered me a ride home. With every word I spoke I could see my father's face darkening in anger.

'You had no business to leave your friend behind,' he thundered. 'Ramu is your friend and you should have refused the ride if Col Naidu was not prepared to take him along.' With that he got me by the collar and slapped me twice with the admonishment, 'I hope you will remember this for the rest of your life.'

And sure enough I have not forgotten...

This incident made me want to know more about my father. As questioning him about his life was unthinkable, my mother was constantly harassed for answers. Even so, only little bits of information emerged. I learnt about his brilliant academic record, about his being misled into joining the Viceroy's army as opposed to the Queen's army (the former was for NCO's and the latter for officers), the rectification of this mistake by a kindly British officer who saw the potential and qualifications of this young man, and the burden of the family being carried by this young officer who had to sleep on the veranda of the officers mess as he could not afford to pay the mess bill. These stories put him on an even higher pedestal.

The other great source of information about my father were the troops that he commanded. Most of the pre-boarding years of my childhood were spent with the troops under his command. As soon as school was over, I would head for the barracks, or at the appropriate time, the 'langar'. The jawans, who obviously missed their families greatly, would welcome me with enthusiasm. I would play games with them, run cross-country with them, cheer them on during different tournaments and often eat with them. Through all this, I would hear stories about my father. How he remained with the troops every step of the way during long route marches, asking for no privilege for his rank, how he dealt with indiscipline with an iron hand and yet how kind he could be when the occasion demanded; how he had rescued a man lying next to a burning oil tanker with no regard for his own life, how fair he was and how he would stand up to even the Brigade Commander for the sake of his men. From those early days I venerated the man, as did my older brother who followed his footsteps and went on to join the army.

My older brother was a chip off the old block. This became

clear when he became commander of a battalion, (incidentally, the same battalion that our father had commanded). His Subedar Major visited me while in Dehradun on his leave at a time when I was teaching in the Doon School. I will never forget what he had said, 'I have been in the Army for close to thirty years but I have never worked for a leader like your brother.'

This idyllic', paltan' life was cut short when I was sent off to St Xavier's boarding school in Jaipur at the age of eleven. This education demanded several sacrifices from my parents but the choice was made considering that the school was close to my father's regimental Centre in Nasirabad (incidentally my birthplace). Therefore help would be close at hand if required. Mercifully that need never arose and I do not recall seeing anyone, (not even my parents), from the regiment, all through my six years at that school.

Ill-informed though the choice of school may have been, it turned out to be the best thing that could have happened to me. St Xaviers was a small school, the boarding even smaller. Unlike most other boarding schools that I happened to head in later life, it was a singularly happy place. And the main reason for this was that bullying did not exist. On the contrary, unbelievable though it may sound, the seniors went out of their way to befriend the juniors. One particular incident remains etched in my memory.

The boarders were playing an inter-house football match. The opposing team had a star player called Chandrasen who was reputed to be one of the tougher students in the school. On our team we had a student called Debabrata (who incidentally shared my surname). He was a quiet, studious kind of person who liked to be left alone most of the time. Somewhere along the line he had acquired the reputation for being the 'strong, silent' type. During the course of this particular football match, Chandrasen seemed to be intent on terrorising the juniors, committing one foul after another against them. Suddenly in the middle of the second half, Debabrata walked right up to Chandrasen, grabbed him by the collar and administered one tight slap with the warning, 'Pick on someone your own size!' A stunned silence enveloped the ground. The referee, one of the Jesuit priests, chose to ignore the whole incident and play carried on without any further hitches.

This was the culture that the Jesuits who ran the place had created, along with a huge emphasis on honesty and integrity. We fought our own battles as long as they did not get out of hand. The school was Christian, but there was never a hint at proselytisation.

There was a great emphasis on hard work and hard play. It is not a coincidence then, that this small, relatively unknown school produced some of the top ranking officers of the defence services, including a Chief of Naval staff, several gallantry award winners, an international basketball player, a Vice Chancellor of Delhi University and three Rhodes Scholars!

The one man who bestrode the school like a colossus, at least for us boarders, was Father Gerald Peter Grace. Father Grace was our hostel superintendent, history teacher and basketball coach, but his presence seemed to be felt in every single area of our lives. If Father Grace had not taken to the priesthood, I think he would have made a first-rate Marine. Like a true Marine, he led from the front by example. If we had to go on a long distance cycling trip, it was Father Grace who would cycle with us every mile of the way. As a basketball coach he pushed us to the limits and would often stay back long after we had left the courts to practise by himself. It was no surprise that the school fielded one of the best basketball teams in the state and took on and beat, teams from the university, the Railways and Defence Services. One of our players, Harkirat Sidhu (now a senior corporate executive), even played for India, as a schoolboy!

Yet it was as a disciplinarian that Father Grace outdid even a sergeant major. He had a no-nonsense attitude and some of the tougher cases would receive a volley of well-placed slaps. Corporal punishment was not a crime in those days and many of us received more than our fair share of what were known as the 'six of the best'. All we did was to rub our sore bottoms, much to the amusement of our friends and swear that we would never attempt the prank again.

While I am certainly not making a case for corporal punishment, the truth is that whether it was Father Grace or any of the other priests who administered the punishment it was never done in a rage or in a spirit of vindictiveness. It was always fair and never excessive and it certainly did not leave us emotionally scarred for life. However the school saw its own share of pranks. I was up to them all the time, so much so that on one occasion Father Grace wrote to my parents, 'We could do without him here.'

There was this one particular incident when things got a little out of hand. Our school used to be invaded by kites, particularly during the lunch recess when the day scholars would pull out their tiffin boxes. There was many a time when a boy would be about to sink his teeth into a delicious parantha when one of these invaders would swoop down from the sky and with unerring accuracy separate the boy from his tiffin.

Our biology master was constantly on the look-out for specimens for his biology lab (unknown to the priests, I suspect) and offered us five rupees for every kite that we delivered to him. This was a princely sum, considering our monthly pocket money was all of four rupees. My mind recoils in horror at the thought of what retribution this act would have invited in this day and age. But life was a lot simpler then.

Some of us had devised a rather ingenious way of trapping kites. When the birds were taking a break from divesting unsuspecting young boys of their lunch, they would sit on the ledges of our classroom windows, with their tails swaying provocatively within reach. During such occasions we would smuggle a laundry bag into our classroom from the boarding house and one of us would take the seat closest to the window, while the other sat at the next desk, laundry bag ready. If the teacher happened to leave the classroom or was late, the boy near the window would grab the kite by the tail and in one swift motion deposit it in the laundry bag which his partner had kept in readiness. A chain of delivery would ensure that the kite was delivered to the lab assistant within the space of a few minutes.

One particular day, when money was particularly short, my friend J. K. Walia and I decided that desperate times called for desperate measures. Our chemistry teacher had turned up on time and unlike other days when he always took a toilet break (to smoke, we suspected) he refused to leave the classroom. JK and I were beside ourselves with frustration as a kite tail swayed tantalizingly by the window seat. Finally it all became too much. As the teacher was explaining an equation on the board, I got up, grabbed the tail and shoved the kite into JK's laundry bag. The teacher was about to turn around at this point, equation having been explained, so JK opened the flap of his desk and shoved the kite in. It all seemed to have gone faultlessly until a few minutes later, when the kite having recovered from its initial shock started a monstrous fluttering inside the desk.

'JK what is that noise?' asked the teacher.

'Nothing, Sir,' said JK trying to look his nonchalant best. 'I have a habit of shaking my legs.' The class hooted with laughter. Suspecting something amiss the teacher walked up to JK's desk and demanded that he open it. JK pleaded that it was unnecessary, but a second round of flapping made his plea redundant. Very reluctantly, as we watched with bated breath, JK slowly lifted the flap. A thoroughly enraged kite, which by now had slipped out of the laundry bag, shot out of the desk and got the chemistry teacher squarely on his face with a wing, knocking off his spectacles.

JK and I were marched to the Vice Principal's office where we received 'twelve of the best'. Needless to add both of us found it difficult to sit for a few days.

These pranks were however fairly schoolboy-ish and harmless. During my tenure as the head of different schools, I came across several incidents which reminded me that my times in school were essentially a time of innocence.

The report card that followed in the wake of this incident, where the school indicated that they might want to part company with me, was however, to become a turning point in my life. When my father read it (I was home on vacation at the time), he took me along for a walk to the nearby government school.

'See that school,' he said. 'The children there study for free, unlike your school to which I pay a better part of my salary. If you choose to carry on in this fashion, this is where you will go in the next academic year.'

I knew my father. He was not bluffing. I was in class nine at the time and as soon as I got back to school I hit the decks running. No more tomfoolery and the grades which had reached rock bottom, began a precarious climb upwards. Years later I asked Father Grace to referee my application for the Rhodes scholarship. Whilst I have no idea of what he wrote, knowing the man, I am sure he would have been very balanced in his judgement, although I was frequently on the mat in his presence.

When I look back on my school life, I realize that it was a hugely formative experience for me. I was lucky to be taught by some great teachers (I went on to do history at university largely because of Father Grace), made some great friends and above all imbibed some wonderful values. The Jesuit priests were remarkable in their dedication. Most of them were either American or Irish and their lives revolved around looking after us.

In retrospect, I guess we did miss having a mother-like figure in the dormitories. One of the direct consequences of this lacuna was poor hygiene. The smell when we took off our socks after games would have driven Osama Bin Laden out of his hideout! The lady teachers in the classroom did try and make up for this gap in our lives, but then they were day time staff and were not available when we needed them most.

Reading was hugely encouraged. There were reading 'preps' almost every day and a well-stocked library to plunge into. The librarian, who was the brother of the then famous film comedian Asrani, was an extremely welcoming individual and for some of us who read voraciously, he bent the rules liberally in lending us more than our allowed quota of books.

Sport was very high on the agenda as well. Basketball, as I have already mentioned, was a very great strength, as was swimming. Though not very good myself, I was useful enough to find a place on the soccer, basketball and hockey teams. And the basics that I learnt about sport and sportsmanship have stood me in good stead all through my life.

One of the boys in school who had a great impact on the way I was to grow up, was a lad called Jai Seelan Velu. Funnily, Jai Seelan was not a friend of mine. As a loner who ploughed a lonely furrow, he was no one's friend. The fact that he was from the southern part of the country in a school set in northern India also made him stand apart in some ways. A loner is hardly ever understood, particularly in a boarding school and so Jai soon became the butt of all kinds of jokes and pranks, which he bore rather stoically.

The annual sports day, perhaps the biggest occasion on our calendar, was around the corner. All of us were busy training for the big day, or rather two days. The headlining event was the cross-country race, since the entire boarding school participated. I had been in earnest training for this competition and was considered a serious contender for the top spot. Jai Seelan was also training and in his typical manner, all alone. No one paid him serious attention.

On the day of the race, we were flagged off early in the

morning by the school Rector, from outside the school gates. I was right up there with the leaders and Jai Seelan was nowhere in sight. As we turned around at Statue Circle, the halfway mark, a slender dark figure strode effortlessly past us, the leaders of the pack. It was Jai Seelan! From that point on, there was no catching him try as much as we might. I finished second, at least a hundred metres behind Jai Seelan who was doing calisthenics for relaxation as we huffed past the finishing line. I cannot remember anyone ever making fun of Jai Seelan again.

There was also a certain simplicity about our life in a boarding environment which doubtless moulded our world view in adult life. Almost all of us who attended St Xaviers, particularly as boarders, were from middle-class families. I cannot remember even one of our parents driving to school in a car, leave alone an expensive one. With our monthly pocket money we all availed of the same goodies in our tuck shop. All boarders were expected to stay in the boarding during term time and there were no exceptions made.

Perhaps the most levelling factor was that parents could not in any way influence the school authorities to seek undue advantage for their child. To begin with, parents hardly ever visited the school. This was partly a function of the times. Few people had cars and travel was difficult. It was also partly because parents had not yet started seeing education as a consumer product. 'I am paying and therefore I am entitled' was not the prevalent attitude. On the contrary there was a considerable degree of reverence for those teaching their children and a belief that the best would be done for them.

The only confrontation between parent and school that I

heard about, and was perhaps apocryphal, was actually quite hilarious. The school had a large number of boys from the Bishnoi community of Rajasthan. It so happened one year that one of the Bishnois who had applied could not be admitted on account of a serious shortage of space in the boarding houses. Thereupon, a jeep full of Bishnoi men drove through the night to the school and confronted the principal with the offer of a wrestling match! If the father of the applicant won, the applicant would be admitted—if not, the application would be withdrawn! Needless to say, Father Pereira did not take on the wager and persuaded the clan to wait for the next session!

In retrospect, perhaps it was too simple and too protected a life that we led in those idyllic surroundings and a rather rude wake-up call awaited us after our school leaving examinations.

2

The Graduate

It was indeed our good fortune that we did our Indian School Certificate (ISC) examinations when we did. If we had achieved the same result in this day and age, I doubt if most of us would have even been allowed onto the campuses of our better, or even lesser-known colleges.

Armed with eleven points in my ISC examination (gained from five subjects, a 'five point' was the ultimate dream), I set off to seek admission to St Stephen's College. The initial application had been successful and I had received an interview letter. My father had been very encouraging, but he was not in a position to either help or accompany me on my quest. By this time my father had retired as a lieutenant colonel from the army and had struck roots in Bhopal, drawn by the beauty of the lakes. There he built himself a rather unusual house, virtually perched on a rock, overlooking the lake from the height of Idgah hills. He had managed to buy this property at a throwaway price. With his typical ingenuity, he created a beautiful terraced garden. Soon 'the rock' became the talk of the town.

And in his typical and (though I hate to use the word) secular manner, he named the house Khwabgah (house of dreams). At Khwabgah, he had settled into his daily routine of gardening, breeding tropical fish, reading the daily newspaper, writing political commentary for *The Statesman*, walking his dog in the evening and then settling down with his two whiskeys to read a good book before listening to the nine pm news on his Peto Scott (c. 1951) radio.

Occasionally, he would venture out to his farm which was about thirty miles out of Bhopal and which he owned in partnership with his Subedar Major and Havildar Major (both retired as well). Whatever time was left over was spent in helping with the local neighbourhood issues. A life so busy and fulfilling was difficult to imagine

His passing away too, was completely in consonance with the kind of man he was and the kind of life he had led. He always said that he wanted to depart without being a burden on anyone. On his last day, he came back from his walk complaining about a stomach ache. My brother had come to Bhopal with the express purpose of taking my father and mother, who, by now had slipped into dementia, with him to Wellington, his own retirement spot, a move my father had very grudgingly acquiesced to. He offered our father medication which was refused in favour of his daily whisky intake. Alas, it was not to be. The pain became worse and by the time my brother could rush him to the hospital, he was gone, of a giant aneurism the doctors said. My brother and I suspect that the prospect of leaving his beloved Khwabgah and the beautiful garden and the tropical fish that he had so lovingly raised, proved all too much. That was his final stand. The final stand of a man who had never in his life compromised his principles, who had the courage to step across a sea of dead bodies and carcasses in the wee hours of the morning after the night of the Bhopal gas tragedy, to walk to the Post office to inform his sons through a telegram that their parents were safe and then turn his attention to help those he could. At his cremation, his man Friday, Arun, quietly slipped in a bottle of scotch and his favourite smoking pipe with him.

'He would have wanted that,' said Arun. 'He lived like a king, he died like a king.'

For me it was a body blow as my father and I, after the distance of the childhood days, had actually become very good friends. His razor sharp mind, his political analyses, his zest for life, his courage of conviction never ceased to amaze me. I had lost a great pillar of support.

St Stephen's was the holy grail and I really knew how much my father wanted me to join that institution. But when he saw me off at the railway station, all he did was to shake me by the hand (he never hugged us) and say, 'Give it a good shot but if you don't make it don't worry. It is not the end of the world.'

Delhi, after sleepy little Bhopal and Jaipur, was quite an unnerving experience. The auto ride from the station to the University was a bone shaker. It was in this shaken state that I entered the hallowed portals of St Stephen's College.

The story inside St Stephen's was totally different. One had to report to a rather avuncular Robert saheb at the office, a portly and benign gentleman who we soon discovered was the pillar that St Stephen's rested on. Robert saheb pointed me in the direction of the room I had been allotted for the night, which I found I had to share with another equally nervous young man from the north-east.

My first introduction to how unique St Stephen's College was, and how different the times were, was on the next day when I was sitting outside the Principal's office waiting to be called for an interview, along with about fifty other candidates. As we were sitting there, a rather distinguished looking gentleman started questioning each one of us about our names, schools and so on.

'That is Amin saheb,' whispered the boy sitting next to me. 'He is a very senior professor here,' he added. Upon reaching me Amin saheb held out his hand for my papers.

'St Xavier's Jaipur? Basketball? First division? *Tumhara admission ho gaya hai* (your admission is done). Collect your papers from Robert saheb.'

And that is how I became a Stephanian!

Talk about culture shock. To be transposed from St Xavier's, Jaipur to the high-powered environs of St Stephen's College and that too in the days of flower power, was a shock indeed. The move from a highly protected and structured boarding school life to the seemingly unfettered freedom of University required a huge adjustment. In fairness to St Stephen's however, with its system of block tutors and, register (i.e. attendance each night) it was as close as any college could get to the safety net syndrome of a boarding school.

Yet with that safety net there was considerable freedom of choice. One could opt to attend class (provided one kept the minimum requirement in mind); one could drop sport or co-curricular altogether (as indeed some with formidable reputations from their schools did, as the gust of the new-found freedom blew them away) or take up an interest with a passion. The first few months for me were ones of bewilderment and anxiety. How was I going to cope with this alien environment? Most of the other students seemed to have a lot more money than I did. My father was on a paltry pension (the pay commissions were a thing of the distant future) and my brother, a recently commissioned officer in the Army, had to dig deep into his meagre salary to support me. It was his large heartedness that got me through this difficult phase.

That is a debt of gratitude which I have not been able to repay to this day, as indeed for his looking after my mother to her dying day—a duty which, for a variety of reasons, including my own struggles on the health and career fronts, I was not able to help with at all.

The culture of long hair, jeans, guitars and motorcycles was completely alien to me. It was not as though everyone in St Stephen's was of that ilk. There were plenty of good old-fashioned 'squares' like me around. Perhaps there were more of us than the other kind. But to me it all seemed so daunting that I felt rather inadequate. It did not help that the gentleman down the corridor from me breezed into my room one day replete with long hair and guitar, sat on my bed, lit up and invited me to have a 'joint'. The only joint I had heard of, being an athlete, were those pertaining to the human body and I was left wondering whether I was being invited to participate in some bizarre cannibalistic exercise!

Although classes and basketball took up a fair bit of time and energy, I found myself slipping into a deep depression. As a matter of fact, within the first three months my mind was made up that I had to return to Bhopal and attend college from the comfort of my home. A dislocated shoulder achieved whilst doing weight training only added to my disillusionment with my condition. My appetite disappeared and I started skipping meals. By the time the winter vacation came around I had managed to lose over twenty pounds in weight. I was not a very pretty sight for my parents when I reached home for the Christmas holidays.

The two weeks or so that I spent at home were understandably spent with the three of us agonizing over my future. My father was very clear in his mind that by giving up an opportunity to be at St Stephen's and trading it for college in Bhopal, I was writing my death warrant as far as a career was concerned. My mother, while she agreed with my father, was torn by the sight of her emaciated son and the thought of his suffering. I have always looked back on that time as a watershed moment in my life. To this day I thank my parents for having dug their heels in. Little did I know then that a whole world of opportunity awaited me because my parents had not allowed me to chicken out.

It was also around this time that I came under the influence of a remarkable man. R. P. Noronha was the Chief Secretary (the senior most bureaucrat) of the state of Madhya Pradesh. Educated at the London School of Economics, he was an officer of the coveted Indian Civil Services. His younger son Ashok, was one of the few friends I had in Bhopal. In those days shikar or hunting was permitted (subject to necessary permits of course) and very soon I started accompanying the Noronhas on their forays into the forest.

The senior Noronha was a stickler for the rules governing shikar. You shot only that which you could eat and only as much as you could eat, you shot only the male of the species where the law so stipulated, you shot on foot and you never left behind a wounded animal. His knowledge of the jungle and jungle craft was phenomenal. It was as close to the legendary

Jim Corbett as you could get.

Though much older than me (he was on the verge of retirement then) RP and I soon became good friends. There was nothing I enjoyed more than sitting with him and listening to him regaling me with not only tales of the jungle, but of his extraordinary experiences as a young administrator in the forests of Bastar. As a young officer he had made a special request to the government to post him to Bastar, when all other officers avoided the place like the plague. He loved to work with the tribals of that area and they in turn worshipped him like a God.

As soon as he retired, RP took himself off to a little village outside Bhopal where he lived in a small hut and was known as the 'Baba'. I spent many delightful days with him there and if today I love my country and particularly its villages so dearly, it is largely because of this wonderful man. He was completely at ease in his village surroundings and the entire village in turn reciprocated the same feeling. Most importantly he taught me how to respect each individual no matter the social status or position.

'Everyone is a genius,' he often used to say. 'You just have to find out what they're a genius at.'

I once tried to justify a poor cop taking a bribe on account of his meagre salary.

'Don't ever justify dishonesty,' RP shot back. 'Once you do that you are on the slippery road to nowhere.'

RP's autobiography, *A Tale told by an Idiot*,' was apparently made compulsory reading for a while in the Indian Administrative Services (IAS) Academy at Mussoorie. He presented a copy of the book to me with the inscription, 'To

Dev, with regards. The Baba says life plays both sides against the middle; and the poor bloody civil servant is the middle.'

As a matter of fact the last letter he wrote was to me from the hospital where he was admitted just before he passed on. It was in response to a newspaper article I had written about him. He wrote to thank me for what he called 'thoroughly undeserved praise'; the last act of a true gentleman.

3

St Stephen's—Rediscovered

Refreshed after my winter vacation I returned to St Stephen's determined to give it my best shot. I hit the books with a vengeance and inspired by that iconic figure, Ranjit Bhatia, (a Maths teacher at college who had been a Rhodes Scholar and an Olympian) I took up in all earnest my quest to be a long distance runner.

It was a fairly calculated decision. I was not very gifted at any of the team sports, nor did I have what it takes to be a racquet player. My dislocated shoulder made basketball difficult. I was desperate to keep fit and Bhatia saheb encouraged me to run with him and his little bunch of runners. Not everyone can be a sprinter and certainly not me, I had reasoned. Yet everyone could be moulded to be a distance runner. Time was to determine how good I could get at the sport.

Soon running became an all-consuming passion. Every moment outside of academic work was spent in either running, or talking and reading about it. St Stephen's had two of the most talented runners in the country at the time in Navin Kamal Juneja and Rupinder Singh, and the latter in particular was a great source of encouragement. As I dragged my weary body over the finish line (and almost always bringing up the rear) in each race, Rupinder and the others would be there with words of encouragement.

At the risk of sounding like one of those nutty American runners out of 'Runners World', running long-distance was more than just a form of physical exercise. There is something deeply comforting, meditative, almost spiritual if you wish to call it that, about the activity. Running along the Ring Road in the early hours of the morning (Delhi was not half as crowded then) was a joyous exercise, giving one time to reflect, ponder and absorb. It was the closest I have come to meditation. Running with a friend too was special. There was no need for conversation. Falling into step with one another required us not to exchange words. Some of us would run from university to Chanakyapuri to see a film, having sent a change of clothes with the less adventurous ones on the bus, not to mention the numerous trips to Bhatia saheb's house in Defence Colony to spend the weekend.

Running also afforded me the opportunity to become involved with a project of a rather unusual nature. One summer I found myself flat on my back in the military hospital at Bhopal where I was admitted on account of a recurring injury sustained because of all the hard miles on the road. When the doctor heard that I was an athlete he told me that the patient in the next room was Tarlok Singh, who had won a gold for India in the ten thousand metre race in the Asian Games at Djakarta. He was sadly enough, dying of cancer.

'Would you like to meet him?' he asked.

I could hardly contain myself at the thought of meeting someone who had been a near legendary figure for us long distance runners, the mystique around him being heightened by his sudden and unexplained disappearance from the scene.

As I sat day after day with the dying Tarlok, the tragedy of his life slowly unfolded itself. After his triumph in Djakarta, he found himself experiencing shooting pains in his spine. The doctors for a long time felt it was a sports injury and treated it accordingly. It was only when the cancer started ravaging him that it was discovered. By then it was too late and he had been shipped off to the hospital in Bhopal for his remaining days. The courage of the man was astounding. He had come to terms with his fate. His only concern was for his two young children in his village in Punjab. What would be their future? As he had not been wounded in 'operations' there was little that the army could do for him besides what was statutorily permissible. But a lot more was required. Coincidentally, this was about the same time that Lilian Board, the 'Golden Girl' of British athletics was diagnosed with a similar condition. In sharp contrast to us, the entire British nation joined hands to raise funds for her. The contrast was shameful.

As soon as I was released from hospital and was back in Delhi, I got our band of runners at the Otto Peltzer Club together and apprised them of the situation. It was decided to take the campaign on a war footing. Every single newspaper was approached with the story and they responded promptly. We got together and organized a relay run from Delhi to Agra for which sponsors paid handsomely. The Madhya Pradesh government, stung into shame by the fact that they were unaware of this happening in their own backyard, made a handsome donation. Corporate houses chipped in. I will never forget my last visit to Tarlok when he grasped both my hands in his and whispered in my ears, 'Thank you for giving my children a chance.' Till date, I have not met Tarlok's children.

I do hope that life has treated them fairly.

It was while I was running that I came across another remarkable individual who was to have a great impact on my life, Dr V.S. Chauhan. VS or Chauhan saheb as he was popularly known, was studying chemistry in Hans Raj College. A brilliant student, he had to chip in with private tuitions while studying himself, to support the family. We met on the running track while training and a great friendship developed between us. Both of us became Rhodes Scholars at St Catherine's Oxford and ran for the college. Today Chauhan saheb is a Padma Shri having retired as a leading scientist for the United Nations in India.

Armed with a passion for running, college suddenly became a challenging voyage having begun as a daunting one. A 'first-class first' in the first year of college, followed by a similar result in the second year, added to my self-confidence. The results of all the miles spent on the road also began to show with the wins in the odd race and a selection to the college cross-country and athletic teams.

The world outside St Stephen's often thought (and perhaps still does) of Stephanians as snobs. Nothing could be further from the truth. We were as ordinary as the person next door. We struggled to find money to go to the coffee house, were constantly in debt, travelled by public bus all over Delhi and lived exactly as every ordinary college student did. There were the affluent amongst us, who rode motorcycles, had girlfriends and frequented posh hotels. This was however not peculiar to St Stephen's alone.

If such labels were true, the Naxal ideology would not have had such a deep impact on the brightest minds of the

College. Those were difficult days and yet they were part of the magic of St Stephen's. Some of our closest friends were drawn into the movement and some disappeared overnight. Many of us fought with the dilemma as to whether we should commit ourselves to the movement or remain distant. In the end we did not and convinced ourselves that it was because we disagreed with parts of the ideology, particularly the violence. But I suspect it was more the lack of courage to take the plunge that held us back.

There were the lighter moments too—the time, for instance when plainclothes men were posted at the coffeehouse. With their typical haircuts, safari suits and bulky shoes they stood out like sore thumbs and became the object of ridicule. Notes were passed on to them through the waiters, which I daresay were far from complimentary and they were openly referred to as 'Big b...lls'. Even in such troubled times, some people had not lost their sense of humour!

Many observers then and some even now said that the Naxal movement in St Stephen's was a fad and that rich bored kids took to it to attract attention. Having been close to some of those who joined, I can say with conviction that nothing could be further from the truth. Misguided they may have been, but each one of these young men believed passionately in the cause, were willing to risk their lives for it and often did. They also happened to be some of the brightest (and wittiest) minds at college and I feel privileged to have known them.

We were also privileged to be educated by the teachers we had. It is rare to come across a single institution where there was such a galaxy of great minds on the faculty. There was

Ranjit Bhatia, who in his own unassuming way was a tower of strength. Amin saheb, the raconteur of medieval Indian history, P. S. Dwivedi (affectionately referred to as 'Pocket Size Dada') with his acerbic humour, who would spend hours engaging us in discussions on esoteric subjects like Asoka's religious policy, at late hours on the wooded slopes adjoining the college known as 'The Ridge'. Dr David Baker, with his meticulous and organized approach to learning; Dr Kalyan Roy Chowdhury in the Economics Department; Dr Bhargava, the affable physicist who was more like a friend; Dr Brij Raj Singh, the brilliant Fulbright scholar who taught English; and Dr V. S. Chauhan, the multi-talented chemistry don. This list could go on and on...

What made the experience even more unique was the relationship we shared with our teachers outside the classroom. We could approach most of them at any time, day or night with our problems (and we did) and we always received a warm and sympathetic response. I remember knocking on Dwivedi saheb's door late one night on the eve of my ancient Indian history examination, in a state of panic. I thought I had a memory blank. In his unflappable manner PSD sat me down, gave me a cup of coffee and said he would ask me twenty questions. If I could answer fifteen of them, I would get a first division, he added. I did and, sure enough, the next day was a cakewalk!

There was also a great deal of humour abounding in the place. 'P. G. Wodehouse week' was celebrated with much enthusiasm and some of the practical jokes were truly memorable. Dolly, the pretty daughter of the head of Department of History, Dr Kapadia, was obviously the subject of much male attention in the college. One year a few intrepid Stephanians hired a band from Chandni Chowk, dressed up a dulha (bridegroom), plonked him on a donkey and brought him to Dr Kapadia's gate amidst much fanfare. To Dolly's credit, she came up to the bridegroom with a charming smile and garlanded him!

The three years of the B. A. programme, which at one time I did not think I would ever have seen through, flew by and before I knew it, I was a graduate and with a second position in the University at that! Hardeep Puri (who went on to enjoy a distinguished career as a diplomat, culminating with his appointment as India's Ambassador to the UN), pipped me to the first place. Very few places that I know of would have supported a lonesome new freshman in the manner St Stephen's did and to me that was (and I hope still is) the college's great strength.

4

The Interregnum

THE SUMMER of 1971 was a summer of discontent. I graduated successfully. Yet knowing that some of the brightest minds of my class could easily have won greater laurels if they so desired, made me question my university rank. The feeling that my accomplishment reflected little intellectual greatness gripped me.

Soon the desire to be financially independent also became a burning one. Not wanting to remain dependent on my father and brother, I packed my bags, informed the College office that I was quitting and set off to Kolkata (then Calcutta) to look for a job. I had a favourite aunt (my mother's older sister) and I was sure she would give me a roof over my head. My assumption was correct. Not only did my aunt welcome me, she also agreed to keep the whole business a secret from my parents. Indeed she went a step further by having one of my late uncle's suits altered by a tailor for forty rupees, to facilitate my job search.

Armed with a hastily put together resume (typed by a footpath typist) and dressed rather nattily, (I thought), in my altered suit, I set off from Fern Road in Ballygunje, to Dalhousie Square, which was the centre of Calcutta's corporate world. The first day I took the tram and that proved to be a near disaster. The crush of passengers did not do too many favours to my suit but thankfully my shoes were spared. It was quite obvious that no self-respecting durwan (gatekeeper) would let me through into any office. So I beat a hasty retreat and from the next day decided to walk the distance.

There was a certain mystique surrounding the corporate or 'boxwallah' culture in Calcutta those days, particularly for the middle-class Bengali. Offices like Metal Box, Dunlop, Tatas, Williamson Magor, were supposed to be the private sanctums of the 'burra sahebs' who reputedly worked in plush air-conditioned surroundings, ate huge company lunches and dined later at the Tolly and Bengal clubs. In this far removed world, I was daring to make an entry.

I must admit that my suit (and perhaps the fact that I did not have a Bengali accent) worked at least with the durwans and I managed to gain entry into most of these corporate bastions, at least up to the receptionist's desk and in some cases up to a middle-ranking officer. In one case I even made it to a Director (because I had read in the in-house magazine at the Reception that he was a Stephanian and I told the receptionist that I was carrying an invitation card for him from college). In most places, however, the standard response was, 'Sorry we have no vacancies at the moment but please leave your resume (called bio data those days) behind. We will contact you at the appropriate time.'

After three weeks or so of relentless knocking on doors, I finally hit 'gold'. Andrew Yule was looking for assistant managers for their tea gardens and this time I not only got past the reception, I qualified for the interview and landed the job! I had no idea what the job involved but in the euphoria of the moment, it did not seem to matter.

The first time my parents got to know of this development was when I took the train back home from Calcutta. They got a shock when they saw me at the door and assumed that I must have been thrown out of college (it was the middle of the term). Once the story was told, there was no disapproval. After a couple of weeks at home I was ready to set off for Dibrugarh in Assam, to join the Rajgarh Tea Estate as an Assistant Manager. In the meantime war clouds were gathering (this was December 1971) and the day before I left, the Statesman issued that dramatic headline: 'It's War!'

It would perhaps not to be out of place for me to suggest that I was one of the first civilians to feel the impact of the war, albeit in a very unusual kind of way. The journey to Rajgarh was a rather circumlocutous one. I had to first travel from Bhopal to Lucknow to take the Awadh Tirhut (AT) Mail to Guwahati before flying to Dibrugarh. Andrew Yule had very generously offered first-class AC travel, and never having tasted that luxury before, I was naturally very excited.

It was decided that I would spend the day at Lucknow with a very dear family friend (also an army officer) before taking the AT Mail to Guwahati.

The first-class AC compartment on the AT Mail surpassed all my expectations. It was one of those old-fashioned ones, rather like a combination of a drawing room and a bedroom with a liveried waiter in attendance. Our family friend, being a senior officer of the army, had one or two men in uniform help me board, whilst he himself strode around the railway platform resplendent in a Brigadier's uniform.

As the train steamed off, I realized I was the only passenger in the luxurious saloon. I settled into the unbelievable comfort of my surroundings with the anticipation of the next two days of this magical journey. Yet what followed was as unsettling as it was comic.

At the first major stop, which was after nightfall, there was a frantic knocking on the door. I hastily opened it and was confronted with the sight of a large crowd comprising mainly ladies armed with garlands, tilak, conch shells—in short, the entire armoury. It seems that a message had been received from Lucknow that an officer was on his way to the front to help in the war effort (courtesy the army send off party). My protestations were brushed aside and I was duly garlanded, adorned with a tilak to the blowing of conch shells, and force-fed copious quantities of sweets.

Worse was to follow. Apparently word had been passed down the line to all the major stops for the train of the impending arrival of the 'war hero', and at each one of these dreaded stops, I was feted in a similar manner. What had promised to be a blissful journey turned into a nightmare. I spent the entire time between stops agonizing about the consequences of being found out. I did want to come clean but who was prepared to listen in the midst of the blowing of conch shells? Moreover, to douse the patriotic fervour seemed a cruel thing to do. Needless to say, by the time I got to Guwahati, I was a shadow of my former self!

The stunningly beautiful tea country which the company car drove me through had a picture postcard-like quality. As indeed did the garden and the bungalow which was supposed to be my abode. In the winter months the place, and indeed life there, seemed to soak in the comfort of the winter sun.

At the tea estate I was sharing the bungalow with another assistant manager, Mike Das. He was soon to become my mentor. His very first question caught me completely on the back foot.

'What the hell is someone like you doing here? I mean with your background why do want to rot here?'

Mike, as I discovered was the ultimate cynic and though I learnt a great deal about planting from him I was determined not to let him get to me. I threw myself with gusto into the business of becoming a planter. The manager, Pulin Bhagwati, was a kindly man and he made it a point to introduce me to all the planters around, but it was apparent to me in a few weeks that this was not the life for me. The planting community was very warm and welcoming but I just felt uncomfortable dealing with plants. I realized I needed to do something with people.

Three months down the line I resigned. The Englishman, David Hurst, who came from Calcutta to see me, expressed deep disappointment and said that I had not given myself a chance. But my mind was made up and in April I found myself taking the hopper flight from Calcutta to Bhopal.

At Bhopal, my father received me rather grimly, which was understandable in view of my uncertain future. I wrote to St Stephen's asking if they would allow me to enroll in the M. A. course commencing in July, adding that I had serious financial problems. Amin saheb wrote back that the college would be happy to have me back, with a full scholarship and a room in Residence. I could have wept for joy!

There were still months left for me to join college. My father suggested that I make myself useful at the farm. He could not have made a more sensible or wiser suggestion. Those few months at the farm, where all I was allowed was what the Subedar Major and Havildar Major allowed themselves, (which was ruthlessly spartan), were a turning point in my life.

I saw a woman worker go off to deliver her baby in the middle of the working day in the bushes surrounding the wheat fields, accompanied by a midwife. I ate roti and onions for lunch (onions were still affordable for the poor in the pre-Sharad Pawar days) and I discovered how tough and resilient village folks, particularly the women, are. While I was not privy to their inner lives, I did experience their warmth and generosity. This little sojourn made me conscious of a life which I had not known existed and rendered me deeply grateful for all that I was privileged to have.

5

St Stephen's—The Second Innings

July 1972 saw me back in the familiar environs of Mukarji West, the residential block in which I had spent my undergraduate years at St Stephen's. My classmates were now those who were previously a year below me. But that did not seem to matter as we had been good friends earlier (and I dare say continue to be good friends even now).

It took a few weeks for me to realize something rather disturbing about myself. While I enjoyed being in St Stephen's College, I was completely bored with academic work. The two years of the M.A. programme were made academically palatable largely by two men, Dr Randhir Singh, who taught us Political Thought and Mr Mohd Amin, who lectured on medieval Indian history. Their lectures were thought-provoking and inspirational, but all the others seemed dull and pedantic.

To me, involvement in all the other areas of life in 'Stephania' became a lifeline out of a state of boredom and ennui. The privilege of being the vice president of the committee of games (i.e. the student heading all college sports) was a huge opportunity. A group of us decided to shake up college sport and make it truly national. The first step in this direction was to organize an all-India swimming meet, in memory of Kiran Seth, a college swimmer who had died tragically in a flying accident.

Our group, consisting of stalwarts like Vikram Nair and the late Pankaj Aggarwal, fanned out across Delhi with an appeal, mainly to the alumni of the college, for funds for the cause. The swimming pool at the National Stadium was hired for three days for this purpose and the Delhi Swimming Federation agreed to recognize our event. Officials were deputed to officiate at the meet to give it the official status that it required. Teams from all over North India were invited and accepted.

Imagine our disappointment when on the very first day, with the competitors all warmed up for the first event, the officials strolled in about half an hour late and promptly began demanding their breakfast packets. It was a sorry situation. Somehow we struggled through the first day's events but it was clear that a repeat performance could not be allowed.

That night volunteers spread out across all the halls of residence on campus. Their mission—to persuade fellow Stephanians to donate for a worthy cause. The cause was to hire buses from Chandni Chowk to ferry 'officials' to the pool in the early hours of the morning. These 'officials' were ordinary Stephanians who had been given a crash course on their duties into the late hours of the night before.

The next morning, as the sun rose, a bus-load of 'officials' was on its way to the pool. The meet started on time, much to the delight and relief of the competitors and the dismay of the real officials who turned up at their convenience. They blustered and threatened not to recognize the meet. We refused to be browbeaten. The meet ran like clockwork for the remaining two days. The recognition we wanted came in the form of a screaming headline on the sports page of the Statesman—'A swimming meet to be proud of!'

The article went on to describe the sterling work done by the young college students and how this was an example to all sporting officialdom. With reluctance an embarrassed Delhi Swimming Association finally recognized our event. The apogee of this event was when the legendary S. K. Bose, a Cambridge philosopher and retired St Stephen's professor sent me a postcard, which I have preserved to this day, writing:

'Dear Devapriya,

It is only fine leadership and excellent team work that could have provided the great show at the NSCI pool yesterday and today. As a Stephanian, I felt very proud and I would like to convey my thanks to you and the others who helped you for what you have done.'

The success of the swimming competition inspired us to host an All-India table tennis tournament, to which we were able to invite the leading table tennis players of the country at the time—our own Deepak Vadhera, Pankaj Butalia, Mir Kasim Ali, Jagganathan and many other leading lights of the sport.

When Bose saheb spoke of others who helped, he could not have known of the help that we received from Ranjit Bhatia, the President of the college committee of games, to whom I reported directly.

Bhatia saheb, as he was affectionately known, was a legend in his own right. A former Olympian (he competed in the Rome Olympics) and Rhodes scholar, he taught mathematics at St Stephen's and was possibly the most self-effacing person I have ever known. Despite his stature, he was always backing us and supporting us, whether it be in the organization of an event such as the swimming meet, or reaching out to us for our personal problems. I remember that a few months prior to my departure for Oxford, I was having difficulty finding a place to stay. Bhatia saheb did what very few people would have done; he welcomed me into his own home. Rani, his wife and he regularly welcomed many a homeless Stephanians like me into the warmth of their family. It was this wonderful bond with a teacher that made St Stephen's so different.

A few months later I scraped through my M.A. Finals, barely making a first division. Today when I hold my M.A. Degree in one hand and Bose saheb's postcard in the other, I know which one I am more proud of.

My postgraduate stint at St Stephen's had also given me a chance to become involved in student 'politics' if indeed one could call it that. The authorities in my final year suddenly decided to introduce a very steep hike in the fee for residence in college. We were told that this was to improve the quality of life for us boarders. We waited patiently for a few weeks to see what areas of our lives would be improved. When nothing of consequence seemed to be on the immediate horizon, a group of us sought a meeting with the Principal, the Revd W. S. Rajpal and the Bursar, Dr Nagpal. The meeting proved to be rather inconclusive, as the authorities did not seem to have any concrete proposals for us. It was therefore decided that classes would be picketed until such time as solid proposals for the improvement of life in residence were put forward. In a college like St Stephen's this was nothing short of revolutionary.

Student opinion, particularly that of the day scholars, was hugely divided. Numerous student meetings were held. There was a palpable buzz in the air, as rumours flew thick and fast. Mercifully, before the situation got out of hand, the College Board summoned a meeting to which some of us were invited as student representatives and the entire issue was resolved in a very amicable manner. Some of the proposed increases in fee heads were postponed till such time as the exact improvements could be identified.

I rather suspect that if the improvements did happen they happened perhaps a few decades after we had left college. The college had been gracious enough to hear us out and that was good enough.

6

At The Crossroads

The M.A. degree had been acquired with a first division (just about), a large number of life skills like teamwork, leadership, crisis management and negotiation skills had been learnt.

What was I to do next, became the question I sought answers for.

In those years, students would enroll for a law degree, secure a room in Jubilee Hall, or some other Hall, for postgraduate residence and set oneself seriously to prepare for the Civil Services examination. This route did not interest me. It was overcrowded and seemed fatigued. At the same time, I had ruled out the corporate world after some agonising soul-searching.

It so happened that S. C. F. Pierson, a retired British army officer and former director of J. Thomas and Company, was a tutor at St Stephen's College. (He found great joy and fulfillment in being a tutor and was always there for any sporting fixture that the college was involved in). A man of means, he took no salary from the college and often invited groups of boys to his quarters and filled them with great food and stories from his younger days in India. Some of us even got so lucky as to accompany him to the Oberoi hotel for dinner.

Stephen Pierson had shown great interest in all that I

had been doing at college. When an offer came along from the Mercantile Bank for a management trainee, he gave me the first pick to it. It was an attractive offer indeed. The offer included two years of training in Hong Kong and then a plush posting to Calcutta with a princely salary and equally enticing perks. I was sorely tempted but something deep down inside kept telling me that this was not the life for me.

Ironically it was Stephen Pierson who settled the matter for me by saying, 'Deva, I have a feeling in my bones that you would be bored to tears with this job. After all for the first ten years you will just be licking postage stamps!'

That decided it.

With these choices not being taken, becoming a college lecturer did not seem to be a bad idea at all. The main advantage would be that I could still keep alive my interest in competitive running. Another round of applications began. The immediate problem was money. Now that the scholarship was no longer available, sustaining oneself was a challenge. As with many subsequent occasions in my life, friends came to the rescue. Vijayan (Unni) Nair, a lecturer and alumnus of St Stephen's, very kindly agreed to share his set of rooms with me. Others loaned various amounts to help keep body and soul together. Mercifully in August, Hans Raj college advertised a vacancy and I made it past a fairly formidable interview to land the job.

They say it is imperative to be well fed in order to have a proper perspective on life. Now that the Hans Raj job ensured that the days of eating 'bun-anda' from the numerous dhabas dotting Delhi University were over, one could sit back and reflect on the direction life was heading in. Yet the feeling of being directionless seemed to have gripped me. I knew that my job as a lecturer was attractive only because of the huge amounts of free time it offered me. The job offered me no motivation. I had no desire to be a professional academic and so this was really a question of marking time. I realized soon that I was in a rut.

But there was one option left, albeit a far-fetched one, the Rhodes scholarship. My dear friend, V. S. Chauhan, had qualified the year before for the scholarship and was at St Catherine's College in the University of Oxford, from where he sent me lengthy letters describing the joys of cross-country running in England. I seemed to possess the qualifications to apply, but how could I compare myself to the alumni of the scholarship which boasted of names like Montek Ahluwalia, Girish Karnad and Aftab Seth? As the spires of Oxford and the green fields of England beckoned, I felt I just had to give it a shot.

The application having made it through the initial stages, I found myself on a train to Calcutta to attend the final interview at La Martinere School in that city. The dinner the night before with the Board was at the Bengal Club. I had only heard stories about its glory and opulence whilst traipsing the streets of the city looking for a job. Now I was actually in it, in the company of some very distinguished people and attempting to win the Rhodes scholarship! The food, which must have been delicious, judging by the fact that it was the Bengal Club, was barely noticed that night. We were taking our leave after the dinner when the secretary of the trust asked us our preference for the slots for the interviews the next day. Anxious to get it over with, I opted for the number one slot.

The next morning I found myself being ushered into

the presence of the luminaries I had only heard of—Lavraj Kumar, India's first Rhodes scholar and a formidable civil servant; Girish Karnad, the famous playwright and actor; Aftab Seth, a diplomat of repute; Ashim Datta, Vice Chancellor of Jadavpur University and also one of the two of India's first Rhodes Scholars; and Mrs Wood, the kindly but intimidating Chairperson.

The interview lasted about an hour. I was amazed at how thoroughly the board had read my application essay and how searching they were in their questions. A huge range of subjects from history to sport, to current affairs, to the condition of our villages, was discussed. The questioning was demanding without being threatening.

And then came the magic moment when at about four in the evening all twenty of us aspirants were assembled and informed of the result. If it had been today, I would have doubtless jumped up and pumped the air with my fist as today's sporting heroes are likely to do. Alas, having seen only Krishi Darshan on a black and white television, all I could do was to raise my hands heavenwards in a silent word of thanks.

The most touching bit came when Ashim Dutta, the Vice-Chancellor of Jadavpur University, bundled the two of us awardees (the second being Desmond Mascarenhas, a bright young scientist from Goa) into his Morris Minor and drove us both to the post office so that we could inform our parents with a telegram. In more ways than one, that little act symbolized the age we then lived in.

7

Oxford Ahoy!

WHILE BEING awarded the Rhodes scholarship was a great honour in itself, the steps leading up to my departure were loaded with significance as well. I was the first person from my family to be travelling abroad and also the first to board a commercial aircraft. In any case, travel, particularly foreign travel, was for most Indians in those days a fairly esoteric, (not to mention expensive) exercise.

The entire family and an army of friends came to see me off at what was then called Palam airport. Even V. S. Chauhan's parents were there and I cannot forget his late father holding me by the hand and saying, 'Please bring my son back.'

As it happened, VSC did come back and how! It is a pity his father is not around to see what a distinguished career his son has built for himself after struggling against such great odds in his youth. My own parents and my brother remained stoic through the farewells, though I could see that my mother was about to burst into tears.

If Palam was bewildering for me, one can imagine what Heathrow did to my system. Very gingerly I dragged my new suitcase (purchased from Jama Masjid for sixty rupees) through the ocean of strange faces and machines to look for the coach service to Reading, from where I had been directed to take the train to Oxford. The first trauma I encountered was the automatic door. As I approached I looked desperately for the handles to open it, never having seen such a door in my life. Incredibly there seemed to be none and yet all the signs pointed in that direction. I could feel all eyes boring into me as I approached the door and I prayed desperately for some divine intervention to help me open it. And lo and behold! Before I could say, 'Open Sesame', the door flew open. I could have collapsed with relief.

Even before I had time to recover came the next blow. The coach for Reading was almost full and waiting. I looked around desperately for a place to park my rather large suitcase but could see none. There certainly was nothing on the roof of the coach, where every travelled Indian would deposit his bags. With no alternative left, I dragged my suitcase onto the bus itself and stood it in the aisle. The other passengers (mainly British) looked up at me with some puzzlement and went right back to their newspaper, crisps or whatever they were engaged in. I continue to stand there, feeling rather foolish as there was not a single suitcase around other than mine. Assistance arrived in the form of the West Indian conductor who with a cheerful, 'Hey man, follow me,' took me around to the back of the bus, which to my utter amazement had a boot! In went the suitcase and yet another lesson was learned about the developed world!

It is very difficult to describe the wave of relief that engulfed me when I got off at Oxford railway station to find my dear friend VS waiting for me. He took me fondly under his wing and beginning with introducing me to all the runners (we were off on a training camp in Wales before the University actually opened), he began showing me the ropes which would help me settle into my new life for the next three years.

Even so more shocks awaited me. St Catherine's, the college VS and I had chosen, (mainly on account of it having a strong cross-country team), was a co-ed college. This was something I knew, but had assumed that as in India, the boarding houses would be a few miles away from each other. What I did not know was that the college had 'mixed' staircases. These were floors in the halls of residence where boys and girls had rooms virtually adjacent to each other. Imagine my horror when on my first morning in the washroom, I found a rather scantily clad young lady brushing her teeth next to me! In my panic I went straight down to the Porters Lodge (i.e. reception) to enquire whether I was in the right college!

Subsequently I was to discover that some of the staircases had condom vending machines. For someone whose nearest foray to the domain of the opposite sex was the back gate of the forbidding Miranda House in Delhi University, this was the sexual revolution brought right to my doorstep!

Dealing with the opposite sex was not the only challenge at Oxford. A greater one was my academic future. I had been accepted into the BPhil programme (a postgraduate degree just short of a DPhil or PhD) based on a paper on medieval Indian history that I had written during my time at Delhi University. By now, however, there were serious doubts in my mind about pursuing an academic career. One option clearly was to do my bachelors degree all over again by enrolling in the programme Oxford is traditionally famous for called the P. P. E. (politics, philosophy, economics). But the thought of having to go through that grind again was not a happy one.

Completely perplexed I turned to the Master (Head) of my college, Lord Alan Bullock, an authority on Hitler and a former Vice Chancellor of the University, for advice.

As I entered Lord Bullock's office I was petrified that he would lambast me for my indecision and for wasting the money of the Rhodes Trust. What I was totally unprepared for was the warmth of his reception and his sympathetic attitude.

'Don't worry, young man,' he said, after hearing of my dilemma. 'You are not the first to graduate to realize that this is not what he wants to do. But cheer up! Oxford has plenty more to offer. There is sports, art, theatre, friendships. And you should drink deeply at all those fountains. As for the academic bit, come back in a day or two and I would have found something suitable for you to do.'

With that he sent me off. Sure enough, two days later his secretary sent me a note informing me that the Master would like to see me.

'I have something tailor-made for you,' Lord Bullock said as I entered. 'Far too many people are obsessed with degrees. You already have two of the finest. So I suggest you do a diploma program instead. It's more earth-bound and will, I suspect, engage you better.'

With that introduction he gave me material on the graduate Diploma in social administration, a two-year programme offered by the Department of Social Studies. It had an interesting range of courses on psychology, British social policy, sociology and also required a small dissertation.

Armed with this material I went to see the warden of Rhodes House, Sir Edgar Williams (Bill Williams as he was popularly known). He was aware of my dilemma and here too the response was sympathetic. 'Get on with it. And just turn up to give me regular updates,' he said.

This led to my turning up at Rhodes House every fortnight for an 'update' accompanied by coffee and biscuits (chocolate digestives were his favourites). That is how I had the privilege of interacting with one of the finest minds at Oxford. Bill Williams had been Montgomery's intelligence officer during the war and Rommel is supposed to have remarked, 'Monty was a fool. It was that Oxford don who won the war for him.' Bill regaled me with stories of the war, of international relations, of intrigue and politics. It was a fascinating learning experience indeed.

8

The Oxford Experience

Once the question of the course that I should pursue was settled, a great deal of calm returned to my life. I could now apportion time for my academic work, my running and my social life.

The academic freedom was marvelous. My courses allowed me to attend lectures of my choice on any given day. I found myself attending some of A. J. P. Taylor's lectures. I had seen his name only on the cover of books. I reported on my weekly essay to my tutor, A. F. Heath, at Jesus College, who happened to be a sociologist of great repute. Add to this the wonderful talks one got to hear from illustrious people from across the world that enriched my experiences. These included Tariq Aziz, the radical student leader who spoke on student movements, South African black leaders who spoke of the struggles of their people, Neil Kinnock on British politics, and Ron Hill, the 'marathon man', were amongst the many who added to the quality of our lives in the University.

With the stifling pressure of the examination system to which I had been subjected to at home having been lifted, learning actually became fun. I distinctly remember I quoted liberally from the great authorities on the subject in my first essay which I had written for my tutor. This was a practice I had learnt in India. My tutor heard me out patiently and then remarked, 'Now that I have heard what the whole world has to say on the subject, I would like to know what Mr Lahiri has to say.'

That pretty much summed up the nature of learning at Oxford.

This one comment was to have a profound impact on my entire approach to life, particularly as an educator. The ability to think for oneself, to make up one's own mind and not be influenced by the sheer weight of numbers, or indeed even authority, was something that the tutorial system at Oxford ingrained into my DNA and made virtually the raison d' etre of my philosophy as an educator.

My college, St Catherine's, outdid itself in the quality of friendships that it promoted amongst its student body. St Catherine's was a relatively new college founded by the visionary Lord Alan Bullock, a man who rose from rather underprivileged circumstances by dint of sheer hard work and quality of mind. 'Catz' as the college was affectionately known, wore its commoner identity fiercely on its sleeve and attempted to break away from the stiff upper class image that seemed to haunt most Oxford colleges. Nowhere was this more apparent than in the annual college photograph, to which students turned up in all kinds of outlandish costumes and struck equally outlandish poses, including some standing on their heads! This fierce espousal of its identity brought forth a great camaraderie amongst the students.

Traditionally, every college in Oxford is divided into three bodies. The SCR or Senior Common Room comprises the faculty, the MCR or Middle Common Room comprises the graduate student body and the JCR or Junior Common Room denotes the undergraduate body. In my final year I had the privilege of being elected President of the graduate body represented by the MCR. In no other college in Oxford was the relationship between these three bodies (and the MCR and JCR in particular) so cordial and easy-going. The undergraduates flocked to the MCR on most social occasions and the reverse was equally true.

Catz was famous for its JCR discos on Saturdays and this event attracted students from all over the university. The JCR of course saw this as a great opportunity to raise funds and a token amount of a pound was charged for each entry. The ticket was in the form of a stamp on the palm.

There was a story, however apocryphal, of how on one Saturday night when a particularly well-known band was playing at Catz, the doors had to be shut very early as the place had become overcrowded. Some students from another college found a ladder and tried to scale the JCR walls and let themselves in, only to find a JCR official duly seated at a desk on top of the wall with his stamp and the request, 'Your pound please!'

In those years, Oxford was notorious for its imbalanced male-female ratio, unfortunately to the disadvantage of males. Catz, being co-educational, did not encounter this problem, allowing for a great deal of mixed company available. While there were definitely a fair number of romantic liaisons (and the authorities had been very farsighted in providing contraceptive vending machines on the staircases), for the larger part the girls were regarded very much as one of the 'chaps'. Not only were they accomplished sportspersons themselves (Catz had a great women's rowing team) they even accompanied the boys for rugby and soccer fixtures. I rather suspect that they regarded the antics of the boys with a rather benign disdain. By far and large, we were great friends and one could easily ask a girl go out to a theatre or a film without it being regarded as a 'date'.

The bar in the JCR at St Catherine's was the centre of the college's social life. Not only was it very well stocked but like most Oxford colleges in those days heavily subsidized. Little wonder then that the atmosphere at St Catherine's intended to be rather bucolic and I must confess that some of my happiest memories are those of sharing a few 'jars' with my friends, either at the college bar or in some beautifully picturesque country pub, for which Oxford is justly famous. There were, of course, occasions when things tended to get a little over the top and out of control, as for instance on the day when we finished our final examinations and had to be carted to the 'School's' dinner (the farewell dinner hosted by each Department for graduating students) in wheelbarrows!

There was also the time, when after I had successfully run my first marathon, I was made to drink (or at least to try to drink) a glass of wine for every mile that I had run. And there were twenty-six of them! Needless to say, I did not (and could not) run for a few days after!

One person who had a bit of a difficult time in understanding the unique culture of St Catherine's College, at least in the beginning, was Benazir Bhutto. She came to the college as a graduate and since I was president of the graduate body that year, it fell to me to allot her a room and welcome her into the fold. There was a bit of drama regarding the room and two of her father's aides spent a considerable amount of time with me trying to persuade me to part with the room that I had as part of my Presidential Quota. I did so after explaining to Ms Bhutto, in the presence of my committee, how privileged she was to be a member of the Catz fraternity. Subsequently, (though she spent a great deal of time outside college campaigning for the post of President of the Oxford Union, an election that she went on to win), she struck up a good friendship with all of us and we often debated subcontinental and other politics late into the night. Many decades later when she was Prime Minister of Pakistan and I was Headmaster of Lovedale, we exchanged letters. Her sudden demise, needless to say, came as a shock to all of us.

The friendships that had been formed in those years have, to the amazement of many who attended other colleges at Oxford, survived to this day. We meet whenever possible (on more than one occasion my wife and I have been flown out to the UK by my friends). We communicate and reach out to each other in times of need. Lord Bullock, had he been alive, would have been very proud of his legacy.

When I look back on my Oxford days, I realize that the greatest gift for me was a complete change in my world view thanks to that amazing university. Like most other middle-class Indians who had never been outside India (and in fact not even to many places within India) my understanding of the bigger world was rather limited. 'You can never really make friends with white people,' was something I had been repeatedly told.

Yet Oxford turned all that on its head. A large majority of my friends were white. But I had equally close friendships with Indians, Greeks, Jamaicans and Africans. Nationality and colour did not matter. What mattered was that we cared for and still care for, each other dearly.

Many years later, when I was back in India, I received a letter from my dear Zambian friend, Chisanga. He wrote, 'As you know, I have been in detention now for thirty-eight months. There have been no charges and of course no trial but the authorities have alleged that I knew of a plot to rescue detainees accused of treason from prison. My treatment is not bad, the physical torture having been discontinued a week after I was apprehended. I hope to have good news in my next letter.' Sadly, that was the last time I heard from Chisanga. To have had the opportunity to befriend someone like him gave me a greater education than any book or doctoral degree.

The other wonderful world that I was privileged to enter while at Oxford was that of running. I had chosen Catz largely because of its cross-country team. I was warmly welcomed into the running fraternity of not only the college, but indeed of the university.

It is even more fortunate that Hugh Symonds and his lovely wife Pauline joined Catz to do a graduate year in education. Hugh was (and is) a marathon runner and a very good one at that. He later went on to become Britain's best Fell Runner (i.e. mountain marathon races) and accompanied by his wife Pauline in a van, did an epic run of two thousand miles in ninety-seven days across half a million feet of mountains including two hundred and seventy-seven Scottish Munros, four English Tops, fifteen Welsh Peaks and seven Irish summits, in order to raise funds for Intermediate Technology, an organization that provided advice and assistance on the appropriate choice of technologies for the rural poor of the Third World. In 1990, Hughes was voted 'Britain's Runner of the year'. The year after they finished at Oxford, at my goading and with my help, both Hugh and Pauline spent a year teaching at Lawrence School, Sanawar. I suspect this stint must have had a great influence on their subsequent decision to raise funds for the organization. While in India both of them trekked through a great length of the Himalayas and fell in love with the country. On their return to the UK, they took up teaching positions at Sedbergh, a beautiful part of Britain dotted with hills. As I pen these pages they have retired and are currently cycling all over the world! And Hugh has successfully battled cancer!

At Oxford, Hugh introduced me to Alan Storey (who was to later become the British Olympic marathon team's coach). Alan set us on a gruelling hundred miles a week training schedule. This often included three training sessions a day. In the beginning, I used to be so tired that I felt that I was going into a depression. Yet the irrepressible Hugh and Pauline would keep encouraging me go past that exhaustion barrier till such time as the body got used to it.

There was plenty of competition. I had a reasonable degree of success, including my first marathon at Barnsley which I finished in two hours and forty-three minutes. It was there that I incidentally met my coach Alan Storey for the first time (he had been coaching me on the phone thus far). The Barnsley marathon was also what I consider, in retrospect, a milestone in my life in more ways than one. When I had announced to my running friends at Oxford that I planned on entering the event, the decision had been greeted with a great deal of skepticism.

'He will never be able to finish, leave alone compete,' was the whisper in the locker room at the end of the day's training.

Some even went so far as to suggest that I might do myself some harm by competing in this race. Almost everyone felt that it was far too premature for me to have a crack at a full marathon at this stage of my running career. The only two people who were supportive were my running partner, Hugh, and my coach Alan.

Guided by the two of them, I embarked on a demanding training program which involved at least a hundred miles of running each week and competing in short races over the weekends. The schedule set was exhausting and the races on the weekends did not yield quite the results I expected. Alan and Hugh, however, kept on encouraging me. 'If you keep at it for long enough you will see the light at the end of the tunnel,' they said. I must confess, I found it difficult to believe their words.

The day finally dawned when I found myself on the train to the friendly little Yorkshire town of Barnsley. The local club which was hosting the event had arranged for me to stay with one of the runners and both Andrew and his wife were charming hosts.

As I lined up at the start the next day along with about three hundred other runners, the runner standing next to me had one look at my singlet and shorts and asked, 'Do you think you will be all right, mate? Can't tell about the weather here.' He must have been a bit thrown off by the look I gave him because I had not seen a brighter or bluer day in India.

The start, as was to be expected, was fast and furious. Alan had advised me to get into a rhythm and stay with the middle runners, which I found myself able to do. At the twentieth mile I found that I had clocked an hour and twenty minutes, which was what I had targeted. All seemed to be going according to plan.

But then, as they say, 'The best laid plans of mice and men....'

No sooner had we crossed the twentieth mile mark, the skies suddenly darkened, a stiff breeze blew into our faces and it became freezing cold. So much so, that after another mile, ice started to form on the road and I found myself slipping frequently. It was physically and mentally devastating. The temptation to pack it all in and lie down by the side of the road was overwhelming.

At the twenty-third mile, as if to put a nail in the proverbial coffin, I found myself staring at a huge hill which seemed to be never-ending. Just then, a bearded figure separated himself from the spectators at the foot of the hill and shouted, 'You must be Dev. I am Alan. That hill is much easier than it looks. And it's only another two miles!'

I did not know whether to laugh or to weep. The legendary Alan Storey who had been coaching me painstakingly for the last few months was there himself for my sake! Surely I could not let him down? So there was nothing other than to block out all the thought of pain and stride out in a determined effort.

The last mile was mercifully downhill and I breasted the tape in a respectable time, (of 2 hrs and 43 mins)—a time good enough to prove the sceptics wrong. As for those last miles, little did I know how useful they would be to me exactly thirty years later when I lay in a semi-comatose state in the hospital with multiple organs failing and Indrani, my wife, whispering in my ear that this was the last mile of the marathon and I just had to come through honourably.

I realized soon that I would never be a great competitor in proportion to the effort that I was putting him. Thus I quit competing, choosing to run for pleasure alone. The twenty mile runs on Sunday with Hugh through some of the most beautiful countryside in the world, with both of us lost in our own thoughts and yet matching each other step for step was as close to a spiritual exercise as I could get. I remember that on a particularly beautiful Sunday morning as I ran through Whytam woods, I prayed that my ability to run should never be taken away from me. Sadly, this was one of my prayers that was never answered.

Oxford allowed me to travel extensively. Backpacking with my rucksack and sleeping bag, I saw a lot of Europe and even travelled to Canada. During one spring break, a few of us (we called ourselves the travelling Commonwealth as we were two Indians, an Aussie, a Jamaican and a Canadian) bundled ourselves into a car and travelled over large parts of Western Europe, staying in youth hostels all through.

It was on this trip that VS, my compatriot from India, showed what we Indians were made of. We had all landed up at the Munich Oktoberfest, which is perhaps the world's largest beer drinking festival. At the table next to us was a rather boisterous group of Bavarians, replete with feathers in their caps, drinking large quantities of beer. The leader was a huge man who kept looking over at our table and making funny comments about us to his friends. After a while VS, much to our consternation, got up and walked over to him and explained to him with a combination of gestures and monosyllabic English that he wished to challenge him to a beer drinking competition! The wager was on who would finish a large stein of beer the fastest. And whoever lost would treat the entire opponent's table to free drinks for the evening.

Our hearts were in our mouths as our skinny young scientist took on the bear of a Bavarian. With the clashing of cymbals, the competition started. The entire beer tent looked on in utter disbelief as this scrawny, bespectacled Indian gulped down his stein even before his Bavarian opponent had reached the halfway mark! Needless to say, we did not have to go back to the youth hostel that night!

Perhaps the most memorable experience was when in response to an ad I applied for the position of a grouse beater at the shooting estate of Glenfiddich, famed for its whiskey. I later found out that a lot of college students had applied for what seemed to be a fun thing to do.

It was fun traipsing over hills and dale, beating out grouse for wealthy millionaires who paid obscene amounts of money for a week's shooting. Within the first week of my stay I had made good friends with Eddie Buchan, the gamekeeper and was promoted from grouse beater to gamekeeper's assistant on the basis of my 'hunting experience' in India. My job now was to drive a Land Rover with a walkie-talkie set coordinating the beats with the gamekeeper and his other assistants. A cushy number indeed!

Soon I developed a great friendship with Eddie and his genial wife Sandra. Eddie swore like a sailor but had a heart of gold. The family in a way adopted me and I went back each vacation to spend time with them. When the time came for me to leave for India, Eddie took off his gamekeeper's jacket (made of handmade tweed and especially patented for Glenfiddich) and presented it to me. I have treasured it to this day.

The Scots are probably some of the friendliest, most hospitable people I have ever known. They are also the world's champion imbibers. One Christmas Eve, Eddie's neighbours (from thirty miles away) drove across to have a 'wee dram' (probably about the equivalent of four Patiala pegs) with us. It became quite the evening and I suspect we did serious damage to quite a few bottles of single malt. Late at night I staggered back to the 'bothy', the little shelter adjoining the keeper's residence, where I was staying, to collapse onto my bed in a stupor.

Later that night, I suddenly woke up to the feeling that there was a presence in the room. As I squinted, bleary and whiskey eyed in the dark, I spotted a rather large dark shape moving around the floor next to my bed. I was convinced that it was either a ghost or some primitive savage animal from the moors come to finish me off. The alcohol in my system seemed to have put a lock on my larynx and my attempts at shouting for help produced only a rough guttural sound. All I could do was to curl up in my sleeping bag and hope that the creature would leave me alone.

After a seemingly interminable wait, punctuated by fitful bouts of sleep, dawn arrived. I peered out from my sleeping bag to see that the monster was my army-navy parka which I had thrown on the wooden floor before collapsing. A strong draft from under the door had made it slide around on the wooden floor! This was mercifully my only encounter with creatures of the third kind.

Yet another fascinating experience was working in an Israeli kibbutz. Once again in response to an ad during the summer vacation asking for volunteers to work on a kibbutz, I found myself on a plane to Tel Aviv. I had been allotted the kibbutz of Sde Boker in the Negev desert. It was, incidentally, the one to which the late David Ben Gurion, regarded by many as the founding father of Israel, belonged. There happened to be quite a few volunteers from all over the world on that flight and we were picked up at Tel Aviv airport and driven to the heart of the Negev.

The next six weeks were a truly memorable experience. The kibbutzniks (as the inhabitants of the kibbutz were called), were from far-flung corners of the world, as indeed were we, the volunteers. The kibbutzniks were also from a diversity of backgrounds ranging from a New York cop, writers, naturalists to doctors and teachers. They had all given up the bright lights to come and live in the middle of the desert and share a communal way of life. There was no concept of private property and activities such as dining and recreation were communal.

We volunteers joined the kibbutzniks in the daily rounds of duties (the roster having been announced earlier) and one could be harvesting olives one day, cleaning the toilet on the other and driving to town to pick up groceries on the next. We ate together in a huge dining hall and took turns at kitchen duty as well. In the evenings we would normally sit around a campfire while someone strummed a guitar and others joined in with a song. I remember one of the South African volunteers murmuring one evening, 'What if the whole world were to be like this?'

But Israeli society, as we discovered, had its fair share of tensions as well. The entire nation lived in a constant state of alertness and it was not uncommon to be hauled out of one's sleep with sirens blazing, to participate in a mock war drill. Military service was compulsory and it was a common sight to see young boys and girls hitching a ride back to their duties after a weekend, carrying their sub machine-guns as easily as their shopping bags.

As the six weeks of our volunteer stint drew to a close, Chris, an Australian volunteer and I, decided to be a little adventurous on the way back. We flew from Tel Aviv to Athens, spent a night sampling the famous Greek ouzo and then took a boat to Brindisi in Italy. From Brindisi we took a night train to Rome, where Chris nearly had his rucksack stolen as we took a quick nap in the park outside the railway station. From Rome a train took us to Munich, where we landed to find that the Oktoberfest was on, but that we had barely any money to spare.

We must have presented a very woeful sight as we sat there thinking of 'beer, beer, everywhere but not a drop to drink,' when a group of Aussie Oktoberfesters noticed us. In a fit of magnanimity (no doubt fuelled by the ample quantities of beer they had been drinking) they decided to host us for the rest of the evening!

The next day it was a rather beery-eyed Chris and I who were back on the road, thumbing a ride. We had just enough money to get across to the UK which we somehow managed and I remember scrounging around for the last penny to buy a ticket from Paddington to Oxford.

The journey back included a lift in a BMW, whose driver fell asleep for a blink on the motorway, and the car crashed into the guard rail of the autobahn, did a 360 degree spin, and miraculously righted itself!

My three years at Oxford had sped by magically and there remained one last milestone in the form of the final examination. In the meantime another anxiety had started to gnaw at me. What on earth was I going to do when I returned to India?

The thought of returning dismayed me enormously. I had had such a wonderful time and forged such a great friendships, that the prospect of giving it all up saddened me enormously. Yet there was that feeling that I needed to get back and do something in my country. Was not that what the Rhodes scholarship was all about?

Confused and conflicted, I turned to my mentor, Lord Bullock. As usual, he had nothing but sheer common sense to offer.

'Oxford,' he said, 'offers you a very unreal life. This is not what it is going to be if you get a job, say, in London. You will be condemned to some crummy bedsit and no one will give a damn whether you are dead or alive. Not to mention the discrimination you will come across—unlike Oxford. Take my advice and go back.'

He went on to add that he had contacts in the Oxford University Press and I might want to work with them when I returned.

I walked out of his office reflecting deeply on the perspective he had offered. I had been so taken up by this wonderful world that I had cocooned myself in, that I had not given reality a thought. After some deliberation I decided to take Lord Bullock up on his offer to help with the OUP.

This led me to meet a truly remarkable man, Ravi Dayal.

Ravi Dayal was the General Manager and Chief Editor of the Indian branch of the OUP and he happened to be visiting Oxford that summer. I received a message asking me to meet him at the home of one of the Oxford dons who was hosting him. The meeting took place in the kitchen, over a cup of coffee that RD (as he was known in the Press), brewed for us.

It was difficult to imagine a less General Manager-like person. Dressed in his trademark kurta and smoking his trademark 'bidi,' RD's interview was more of a freewheeling chat than an interview. At the end of it, when we were washing the coffee cups he said, 'Meet me in Delhi when you get back, and we will see what we can do.'

I thus had the comfort of knowing that a job probably awaited me in India.

Examination week arrived. Dressed in the traditional sub-fusck (Gown and mortar board), I trotted off daily to clear the final hurdle. When the result was declared, I had attained a Distinction!

Nobody was more surprised than myself. Sir Edgar Williams too had to take a walk to the Examination School to satisfy himself that the news was indeed true. Later, he dropped me a note in my mailbox at Catz, '*I write to say how glad I am about your Distinction which I saw when I was looking at the notice board in Schools yesterday. You certainly buckled to it in the last year and I will be writing to Ranjit Bhatia to tell him of your success.*'

A few days later as I was packing my suitcase, I received a message from Lord Bullock's office asking me to meet him.

'I thought I would say goodbye to you as I am leaving for a conference,' he said. 'And here's something that you might find useful,' he added, handing me an envelope. Armed with this glittering prize, I headed back to India. And this is what the envelope contained:

From the Master · St. Catherine's College · Oxford · OX1 3UJ

Telephone 49541

Mr. Dev Lahiri has just completed three years as a Rhodes Scholar at St. Catherine's College in the University of Oxford. He has won golden opinions from all who have met him for his friendliness, reliability and good judgment. He was a very popular President of our Graduate Common Room and has contributed a lot to the College during his time in Oxford. He has high standards of behaviour, would be at home in any company and has always impressed me by his integrity of character.

I should be glad to have him with me in any enterprise which called for strength of character and the stamina of a long distance runner, a sport in which he has excelled.

I am glad to recommend him to any employer or institution, and believe they would be fortunate in having him as a member of staff. I should be glad to answer more specific questions in addition to this general testimony.

Alan Bullock

The Rt.Hon. Lord Bullock, F.B.A.
Master of St. Catherine's College
Vice-Chancellor of the University
of Oxford 1969-73

30 June 1978

9

Barsati Days

OXFORD PAVED the way to the Oxford University Press (OUP) in Delhi. These were two different worlds. Situated in the heart of Delhi's Daryaganj on Ansari Road, the OUP office was a far cry from the dreamy spires of the University it represented. One entered it only after negotiating several back alleys. The office itself was rather dingy and functional and one could never guess that some of the brightest minds in the country were hard at work here, honing and polishing the products of some of the finest intellectuals in the world. In those years, OUP India had the finest editorial team in the country.

This team had been put together by none other than the redoubtable Ravi Dayal, who was to be my boss for the next five years. Slightly built, with aquiline features and a rather majestic flop of hair, 'RD' as he was known in the office, was the doyen of publishers in the country. An Oxford man himself and gifted with a razor-sharp mind, RD could smell a good academic manuscript from a mile away. Add to that mind a great love for and understanding of India and it is not difficult to figure out why this man had been able to gather around the OUP banner one of the finest collections of academic authors in the world. With his graceful intellectual charm, RD had the ability to win an author's complete trust and work in partnership with him or her towards producing a first rate manuscript.

It was indeed a privilege that this man took me under his wing and started grooming me in the art of editing a manuscript. Though a demanding boss when it came to professional expectations, he was kind and considerate beyond measure. It was my good fortune indeed that I landed my first job in India, after my stint at the University of Oxford, under him.

Publishing, however, in those days was pretty much of a cottage industry when compared to the rest of the corporate world. Profit margins were very low, especially with an educational publisher like the OUP and the salaries were quite laughable. I joined the Press at a little over a thousand rupees a month and out of this had to finance the tiny little barsati (a small shed-like room on the roof of a large house) that I had moved into in Defence Colony. The location of my accommodation was a strategic choice. I wished to be close to Ranjit Bhatia and his family, be able to take the chartered bus that took me to office and be close to every convenience which I needed at that time.

I had to contend with the social loneliness that seemed to slowly grip my life. After the invigorating social environment at Catz and at the university, life in Delhi seemed to be trapped within what RD facetiously called 'the tyranny of the chartered bus'. My life revolved around catching the bus in the morning and having it deliver me at the bus stop near home, in the evening. Since finance and culinary skills were both very limited, the evening meal was either something scraped off the greasy pan of the roadside stall, or at the height of culinary adventure, an omelette or scrambled egg made on the little shelf of the Barsati, which doubled up as a kitchen.

This lifestyle was a huge shock to the system especially when contrasted with the three sublime years in England. While I was missing the camaraderie of my wonderful friends, the misery of this spartan lifestyle was akin to salt being rubbed into the wound. Had it not been for the warmth and conviviality of the office, I daresay I would have given up.

Someone must have heard my prayers because one fine day in walked into my life Aloke Roychowdhury and his wife, Parna. Aloke was OUP's chief educational editor, responsible for the publishing of textbooks and had been based in Kolkata. The management felt that it would be good for the Press if he were to be moved to Delhi.

The first time I met this couple and their impish little daughter Muniya was when I was helping them move into their flat. Their warmth made me feel like I had known them forever. The Roychowdhurys were a balm on my troubled soul. By this time OUP had been generous enough to grant me a loan to purchase a motorcycle, so every evening I would make a beeline for the Roychowdhurys, often directly from the office. Parna was, and still is, one of the best cooks of my favourite Bengali cuisine and over a convivial drink and dinner, we would converse late into the night. Aloke was an aficionado of literature and films and we discussed amongst other things books, movies and politics.

I also travelled on office work with Aloke, particularly to the north-east, and it was on one of those trips when we stopped off at Calcutta for a few days that an event occurred that was to change my life.

10

The Winter of '79

In November 1979, Aloke (ARC, to give him his office name) and I had been travelling in the north-east and had stopped off at Calcutta. My brother and his wife happened to be there at the time (my brother's in-laws were from Calcutta). One evening my brother phoned me at the hotel I was staying at and suggested that I accompany him and his wife to visit a family friend.

Ever since I had started in the OUP, there were occasions when I experienced great bouts of loneliness. Delhi, as I was discovering at the time, was not the easiest of places for a single person to be in especially when one had just parachuted in after being away for several years. Parties seemed to be the only place for interaction with the opposite sex and I, for one, was way beyond that stage. There were, at that time, no clubs or societies where people with similar interests could meet.

Knowing of my situation, my parents and my brother had often approached the subject of matrimony. An arranged marriage in the typical sense of the word was completely unthinkable for me. But I was getting around to the stage at which I perhaps would not mind being introduced to the right kind of person. As a matter of fact, I had done it for a friend while at Oxford.

This was the background to that particular evening's social call. The family friend in question was a retired Brigadier and he happened to have a daughter who was studying for her Master's degree. Unfortunately, no one had told the daughter the purpose of our visit and it was only after we left that she was asked by her parents her opinion of the young man. She was not sure which one they meant, my brother or I! As for me, I was pretty upset that she had been kept in the dark and that she had been thrown off in the midst of her preparation for her Masters finals. So I called up the family, sought an appointment and arrived the next morning to apologize to the young lady. The rest, as they say, is history.

Realizing that a long distance relationship would not work, I begged RD to have me transferred to Calcutta. The real reason was never disclosed, although I have a strong suspicions that RD had guessed. I arrived in Calcutta before Christmas, proposed on the 25th of December and on 31st Indrani and I were engaged at a wonderful gathering at my friend Surojit (Bunt) Ghosh's home in Calcutta. Bunt and I were old Catz buddies and some other friends from Catz including Larry and his wife Jane and Richard McGow also attended. Of course, the ceremony had to have a Catz twist to it, so my good friends quietly removed the engagement ring from its box and replaced it with a bottle-cap. Imagine my shock when at the magic moment of midnight I opened the box to slip the ring on! Fortunately, Bunt rescued me right away!

As neither of the two families (Indrani's and mine) believed in a long engagement, Indrani decided to drop her Masters finals for that year and we were married in February. A whole new chapter of our lives was about to begin.

11

Married Bliss?

Whoever coined the phrase 'marital bliss' has never tried to live on an OUP salary (of those days) in a city like Calcutta. When Indrani and I looked around, we found that even the pokiest accommodation cost half my salary, if one could manage to find such poky accommodation, that is. After much hunting we settled for a room and a half in an alley that revelled in the name Shyama Charan Sriti Tirtha Lane. The weight of the name and the rent was perhaps too much to bear in that early stage of our married life and so we soon moved to the more salubrious surroundings of Graham's Land, located right behind Calcutta's Tollywood. The accommodation was not a very great improvement, but our neighbours certainly were and we found ourselves living below a wonderful family called the Banerjees who had no hesitation in making us part of their own family.

Professionally those years were not my highest point... I could not fit into the Calcutta office and there clearly did not seem much that I could contribute to. Indrani too was having a hard time. Having had to postpone her final year of Masters at University, she now started looking for a job. The most easily available ones were of a secretarial nature and so she had to enrol in an institute called Dunfords, which had for years together acquired the reputation of producing Calcutta's best secretaries.

To get there and in fact to get anywhere in Calcutta, meant hanging on for dear life to one of Calcutta's buses. And Indrani did everyday what I never had either the courage or inclination to do. She did eventually land herself a secretarial job which meant that we could live a little better than we had been. We even acquired a dog, a Doberman called Razia and this was the beginning of a lifelong passion. It is a huge tribute to Indrani's perseverance that she completed her Masters in the midst of all this chaos.

When the OUP management decided to transfer me to Madras, I saw it as a wonderful way out of the rut that I was in. The sequence of events on the day of our departure should have warned me about how wrong I was on that score.

Indrani and I had set off from our house to the railway station in a taxi with all our worldly belongings (nine suitcases and a dog), to catch the Coromandel Express to Madras. Indrani's family followed in their car. To our horror we found that the main road connecting to the railway station was blocked off owing to the outbreak of a fire in the vicinity. The only way to get to the station was for Indrani to take the suitcases across by the ferry and for me to walk our dog across Howrah bridge. Given that we were fast running out of time, we had to almost sprint to get to the station. To make matters worse, in the rush for the ferry, Indrani was nearly crushed in the mad stampede to get on board. And the ferry nearly capsized on the way! My sprint across Howrah Bridge, with our dog Razia, was a relatively tame affair.

If the departure for Madras was a bit of a disaster, my

stint at the OUP there was an unmitigated one. There was no editorial work to be done and the manager seemed to be marking the days off for his retirement. Indrani, after a great deal of struggle, found herself a job in the local school with a salary that just about paid our newspaper bill. It was clearly time to move on.

As if in answer to my prayers, Hindustan Lever Limited (HLL) advertised the position of an Assistant Communications Manager. The necessary qualifications seemed to fit my profile and it seemed to me to be a big break into the glamorous corporate world, with its fabulous salaries, entertainment allowances, five-star hotel stays and perks. I applied, was interviewed in Bombay, and was offered the job.

RD was upset on hearing about my resignation. He flew down to Madras to persuade me to change my mind and indeed made an offer to take me back to Delhi. I was adamant. This was the big break I had been waiting for. Had I known what awaited me, I would probably have accepted RD's generous offer.

12

The Corporate Bubble

Even as we were packing to leave Madras and take up my assignment with HLL in Bombay, I received a telephone call from the personnel manager (Human Resource these days), who suggested we meet for dinner at one of the city's better-known hotels. I assumed that he wished to talk at length about the assignment.

I was not quite prepared for what followed.

The communications job, the personnel manager informed me, had to unfortunately be given to someone else for various considerations. I was, therefore, being offered the position of Area Sales Manager. I sat there aghast, my jaw dropping. Nothing could be further from my mind then than a career in sales, particularly of consumer goods. As a matter of fact, both the jobs had been advertised on the same day and I had applied after much thought for the communications position.

'Don't worry,' the gentleman assured me over what was now a completely unpalatable dinner. 'Our assessment tells us that you would make a first-rate Area Sales Manager.'

I nearly choked on my dessert.

I knew in my heart of hearts that I was not cut out for consumer marketing. As there was no option, I dropped Indrani and the dogs (by then, in addition to Razia, we had a mischievous little cross-breed called Bo, as in Bo Derek, because she too had an aversion to clothes!) off at Bhopal with my parents and moved to Delhi for a three-month training programme.

My immediate boss in the Delhi office was an extremely likeable young man called Vindi Banga. A topper at both the Indian Institute of Technology and the Indian Institute of Management, Vindi Banga later rose to the top of the HLL hierarchy. Even in those early days everybody in the office spoke of him as being on the fast track.

Apart from being professionally very sound, Vindi was a wonderful human being. He listened sympathetically to my story, but encouraged me to go out into the field for training, adding that I might just end up liking the job.

Alas, that was not to be. The next two months or so were incredibly difficult ones. I could muster just as much enthusiasm for selling soap as a Jain for eating meat. While I admired the company's professionalism, the work ethic of its employees and its rigorous training programme, I could not but help feel totally out of place in this situation. I remember distinctly that at one of the companies seminars in Delhi, the head of marketing got up and announced loudly to the accompaniment of much cheering, 'Gentlemen, this is the year of Rin!'

My heart sank to my boots. I was reminded of a Woody Allen film, where in one scene there are millions of white sperm cells descending a tube, with one solitary black one amongst them. And the black one looks around and shouts, 'What the heck am I doing here?'

It was now just a question of time. And that time came

one day when on the spacious lawns of the Carlton hotel in Lucknow, I sat under a huge tree and much like the Buddha (except that I was sipping a bottle of beer), gained enlightenment.

I had to resign. I put in it a 'trunk call' to Vindi Banga, who very kindly offered to come out to Lucknow to talk to me. I dissuaded him from doing so, as it would be a waste of time and money. My mind was made up. The next night I took a train to Delhi and was at the office with my resignation. Yet another chapter had closed. And a new one was about to begin.

13

Crossroads Again

'WHAT AM I to do next?' was a perennial question in my life. Somehow I just could not seem to find that something which would grab me by my throat. Most people I knew were quite aghast that I had kissed goodbye to a lucrative career in the corporate world. Yet there were two things that I was most definitely looking for in a career. That it be worthwhile, where I could touch people's lives, and that it be fun as well.

'What better option than teaching in a boarding school?' said Shomie Das, as we chatted in the drawing room of his beautiful bungalow at Lawrence School, Sanawar. I had come to know Shomie when I used to go up with the St Stephens athletics team for fitness training at Sanawar.

The man had a great impact on me. I admired him for the effortless manner with which he dealt with young boys and girls and how obviously he was enjoying every moment of what he was doing.

Years later, I was able to work under him in Doon School and Shomie became and still remains for me, a role model in the world of education. Now, at this crossroads in my life, he seemed to be the ideal person to turn to for advice and so I made my way up the mountain to see the man himself.

Both Shomie and his wife Pheroza were extremely warm

and welcoming. 'Let me warn you,' said Shomie. 'There is not much money in it, but it is a great opportunity to mould young, minds. As for fun, I cannot think of a job that provides more if you like being with young people, that is.'

I reflected on what Shomie was saying and it seemed to me that I was beginning to see the light. As I said farewell to Shomie, he added, 'And there is a place in Sanawar for you, should you want it.'

Back in Delhi (we were staying with my brother who was posted at the army headquarters) we debated the pros and cons late into the night. My brother was extremely supportive and felt that what Shomie had suggested was a great option, as did my sister-in-law and Indrani. My only fears were, no matter how wonderful the choice, would I be able to live in the relatively isolated environs of Sanawar? Would the money be enough for us?

As for the first anxiety, a very dear friend suggested that I not take up too many challenges at the same time. Since I was teaching at a school for the first time, he suggested why not try it out first in a relatively more urban environment such as Dehradun? As for the second, the greatest allayer of my fears was Indrani. 'Both of us will work,' she pointed out, 'and whatever the money, I am sure we will manage.'

Soon we found ourselves on the night bus to Dehradun, where a friend had secured an appointment for us with Gulab Ramchandani, the Headmaster of Doon School. The next morning, while attending the Assembly, I received a pleasant surprise when I saw that two former Stephanians and old friends, Sumer Singh and Arun Kapur, were teaching in the school.

Our appointment with Gulab Ramchandani was not until a little after Assembly. So we decided to stroll around and take in the campus in the meantime. The campus was in full bloom in the March of 1983. As we walked along the leafy avenue in front of the Headmasters residence, both of us looked at each other and as if reading each other's thoughts exclaimed, 'This is it!' Something about the day, about the serenity and beauty of the campus, acted as a balm on our troubled souls. We knew where our futures lay. GR (as Gulab was known) was far more circumspect about the whole thing.

'You guys from corporate backgrounds. I really don't know whether the lifestyle and the money will suit you.'

He could not dissuade us. Within a week we were back on campus with all our worldly possessions in a truck.

At the age of thirty-two I had signed an appointment letter which made me the junior-most teacher in Doon School and offered me nine hundred and fifty rupees a month. This was much less than the four thousand on offer from HLL. Indrani was to pick up a job in a few weeks time at Cambrian Hall, a day school close by, where she was offered about eight hundred rupees a month. Both Sumer and Arun cheerfully informed us that we would be broke by the middle of the month but we could not have been happier.

Of course there was a medley of voices around which warned us of our stupidity. 'I give him six months maximum,' said a good friend. But the voice that echoed in my head was that of Biloo Sethi (then India's golf captain), whose advice was repeated to me by another friend.

'If you love something and are good at it, and only a little voice inside you will tell you if you are really good at it, then do it. The money will fall into place on its own.'

I took that advice to heart and have never regretted it for a moment. Years later I was able to repay my debt to that great golfer, when his grandchildren applied for admission to Lawrence School in Lovedale, which I was then heading.

14

Doon Days

At thirty-two, right at the bottom of the food chain, my career at Doon School began with a feeling of being a 'fresher' in college. These feelings of doubt and trepidation were allayed by the the generosity and warmth of my colleagues.

Viji Hensman was the Housemaster of Kashmir A, the house to which I was attached. A kinder or friendlier soul was hard to imagine. In the moments I had to seek advice, I could also turn to stalwarts like Sheel Vohra, RP. Devgun and Sumer Singh any time.

The boys, I daresay, were very forgiving. When I think back on all the mistakes I must have made in those early days of teaching, I shudder in embarrassment. To their credit, the boys never took the mickey. I think what helped was the fact that I was a passionate sportsman and could on a good day, outrun most of them.

When I look back on those nine years in Doon School, I do feel that professionally (i.e. in terms of classroom teaching), we were not perhaps in the same league as some of the teachers of today. Then again teaching as a profession had not really evolved at the time. Schools such as Doon relied heavily on teachers with good communication skills, which is really only one of the skills that go to make the whole package. As in cricket, those were the day of the amateur gentleman.

Where Doon School scored hugely above other schools, was in the quality of student-teacher relationships. Teachers at the school genuinely cared for their wards and their homes were open day and night to any boy who was homesick or troubled or just wanted a bite to eat. And many of us were very fortunate in that our spouses were equally involved in the welfare of the boys. Playing sports together, weekend outings and mid-term breaks contributed to this unique bonding between the teacher and the taught.

While we may not have been as evolved as the teachers of today, there were a few things I learnt at Doon School which were to stand me in good stead later. The first perhaps was the freedom given to teachers.

There was never any snooping on teachers and no one ever dictated to a teacher how he should be teaching. The downside of this was that there really were no structures and this without doubt was abused by some of the faculty.

The other great virtue of both the Headmasters I worked under, Gulab Ramchandani and Shomie Das, was that one could express a dissenting view and it was never held as a grudge. In fact, differences of opinion were welcomed. There was a fine distinction between the personal and the official and never was a difference of opinion on official matters mistaken for a personal attack. I remember once handing in what was tantamount to a resignation letter to GR and all he did was invite me home for a drink in the evening where everything was sorted out. It was not as if there were no differences of opinion within the faculty. The boys were well aware of these differences. One section of the faculty was referred to as the 'paan-bidi gang', and another was referred to as being the residents of 'Prem Nagar' (as there was little love lost between them). Yet I never recall experiencing any vicious politics of the kind that I was to see later in other schools.

Teachers could express their opinions freely at faculty meetings called Chambers. There was this one memorable incident involving one of the stalwarts on the faculty, AN Dar. There happened to be a fair bit of debate going on amongst the faculty on rates being charged for private tuitions during the vacation. Some of the faculty felt that there were those amongst them who were either charging too high or sometimes even too low a rate and that the school should intervene and fix a standard charge for all. When this issue came up in Chambers, AD (as AN Dar was known), put up his hand to take the floor.

'Headmaster,' he said, 'tuition is quite akin to prostitution. Whosoever feels their wares are better, will naturally charge more!'

Needless to say, the issue never came up for debate again.

The boys also taught me one very important lesson; that is not to take oneself too seriously. There were two brothers, Amim and Karim Ahmad, who I remember very well in this context.

Amim was the older of the two and I used to teach English Literature to his class. We had a system of evening classes once a week on Wednesdays. On one particular Wednesday, it so happened that Mrs Mady Martin (wife of the late John Martyn, an illustrious ex-Headmaster of Doon School) had invited us for dinner. To save time, I decided to wear my formals (suit) to class that evening, quite a change from what I usually wore.

Halfway through the lesson, Amim put up his hand and asked, 'Sir, if you don't mind may I ask you a question?'

'Certainly,' I replied. 'What is it?'

I was fully expecting to be quizzed about 'King Richard.'

'Sir, why are you in disguise?'

The class broke into peals of laughter. I was obviously not on the list of the best dressed masters in Doon School.

A few years later it was Karim, Amim's younger brother. He turned up late for class and claimed that he had been in the school hospital getting his athlete's foot treated. However, he was not carrying any documentation from the school doctor to that effect. On being asked for an explanation he replied,

'But Sir, Maa'm (meaning Indrani) was there as well. She will bear me out.'

'And what was Ma'am suffering from?' I asked hoping to catch him out.

'Athlete's wife,' was the prompt reply!

With the professional fulfilment that came with the job, it was not surprising that it was at Doon that we decided to raise a family. Our older daughter Diya was born on 20th January, 1984 and the younger Shama on 22nd July, 1987, the latter under very trying circumstances as within twenty days of the delivery I had to be hospitalized by the first of what were to be recurring heart problems.

Both were born at Luthra's Nursing Home, across the road from Jaipur House. The math was very simple. We were paid eight hundred rupees a year as a medical allowance. If we did not spend the allowance in one particular year, we could afford to have a baby because that was the exact cost of the delivery at the nursing home.

Diya and Shama spent their early years in the idyllic and secure surroundings of Doon School where they were surrounded by many children of their age and of course, the boys, who spoilt them thoroughly. It was not unusual for a group of boys to spend an evening babysitting the girls while doing their homework, while Indrani and I were off at some social engagement. It was truly like a giant family. By then we had also included in our family Bagheera and Ghazal, two Dobermans (plus of course the inimitable Bo) and so it was quite a menagerie. We could not imagine a happier set of circumstances to bring up our children in.

Indrani had acquired a job teaching in a nearby day school called Cambrian Hall. Her second income was critical for our sustenance. When I look back on those days I find it difficult to believe that she managed our lives and her work in the manner that she did.

She would leave for school early in the morning after having got the girls ready for their day, gulping her breakfast down as she rushed off. The girls would be handed over to the part-time 'nanny' who would arrive just in time and the exercise reminded me of that popular party game 'passing the parcel'! She would tear back after lunch to relieve the nanny and bring with her mountains of homework and tests to be corrected. After having spent time looking after the girls and taking them out in the evening she would feed them, bathe them and put them to bed, before burning the midnight oil with her school work. How in spite of this frantic schedule she found time to feed and provide emotional succour to my students and occasionally entertain our friends, still mystifies me. Not a single boy who came to visit went back without getting some 'goodies' to eat, or emotional support if he needed it.

It was also at Doon School that two milestone events (albeit of differing natures) occurred in my life. The first was my participation in the Agra to Delhi run organized by Air Vice Marshal (AVM) Aiyer of the Indian Air Force to commemorate Air Force Day. AVM Aiyer was himself a passionate runner and, at his age, a great role model for the entire running fraternity. His son, Parmeshwaran Aiyer, was an alumnus of Doon School and for some time the District Magistrate of Dehradun.

AVM Aiyer mooted the idea of a group of athletes running from Agra to Delhi, a distance of about a hundred and sixty miles in four days with the runners entering Delhi on the morning of Air Force Day (1st October) as the celebrations got underway. I was privileged to be invited to run along with great runners like my mentor Ranjit Bhatia and some of the top athletes of the country. It was gruelling and had it not been for the superb backup of the Air Force, (which included copious quantities of beer at the end of the day), I doubt if we could have completed it. We ran forty miles a day (twenty miles in the morning and the evening each) and entered Delhi as the jets roared overhead to kick off the celebrations. It was a great achievement and had taken several hundred miles a week of running to be in shape.

The other milestone, though paradoxically also associated with running, was of a different nature altogether. One evening in 1987 (Shama had been born just 19 days prior) I was running with young Bhavnish Marwah, a talented young athlete at Doon School. We were doing some laps of the main field, when all of a sudden, I felt a severe constriction in my chest, accompanied by nausea and sweating. Soon I had collapsed on the running track. The boys quickly lifted me and took me across to the school hospital.

Dolly Dubey, the nurse, took one look at me and realized that she was dealing with a heart problem. She quickly pumped me with some lifesaving drugs, bundled me into the school ambulance and rushed me off to the Doon hospital. The ambulance put up a good fight against the odds in 'Suicide Alley'; the infamous bottleneck connecting us to the centre of town and somehow I got to the hospital alive.

The usual round of investigations, tests, poking and prodding began. And it was the usual result. All inconclusive. The doctors were inclined to think that the episode was linked to the heart but were not quite sure. Medical science had not quite made the kind of advances that it has done today. A few months later, therefore, I did what any self-respecting runner would do under the circumstances; I ran in the Rath half-marathon in Delhi!

I had suffered through the episode indeed. The standards of hygiene in the Doon hospital left much to be desired. I woke up one night to find a mouse negotiating my IV drip! My suffering, however, was nothing compared to what Indrani had to go through. Our younger daughter was barely nineteen days old at the time. Indrani had taken unpaid leave from school as there was no system of maternity leave in those days. We were crippled on one salary and so she had to get back to work as soon as possible. With a baby to nurse and a sick husband to look after, it was a harrowing time for her. Had her parents not come down from Calcutta (travelling unreserved), we would have found ourselves up against an insurmountable wall.

But every cloud has a silver lining. As I lay there in the hospital, tubed up to my eyeballs with Indrani by my bedside, desperately trying to make sense of the jargon that was being hurled around by the doctors, in walked into our lives Dr and Mrs Pandhi. They had two sons studying in Doon School and the younger one, Ajay, used to run with me. Florence (Mrs Pandhi) was a trained nurse and in her own lovable, imperious way, just took over the business of explaining to us what doctors were trying to say. It was uncomplicated layman's language and could not have come at a more opportune moment. This was the beginning of a relationship that has lasted to this day.

The other couple who 'stole' into our lives were Brig and Mrs Mathur. I used the word stole, because each morning when I woke up and peered through my swollen eyelids, I would find either Brig or Mrs Mathur sitting quietly by my bedside and welcoming me back to the world of the awake with a wonderful hot cup of chocolate. Their son Rathin was to later become my student and he has done us the singular honour of naming his daughter after mine (Diya) and his son after me (Dev). Indrani insists this is because it gives him a chance to soundly chastize his son whilst using my name and thereby gaining great vicarious pleasure and revenge for all that he suffered at my hands. Then there was 'Bobby' (Ajay) Hari, an alumnus of Doon School with whom we had become friends. Bobby stood like a rock beside us through those trying days (and nights) at the Doon hospital and indeed later as well. Here again was the beginning of a friendship of a lifetime.

The culmination of my tenure at Doon School was when

I was elevated to the position of Housemaster of Hyderabad. Those were undoubtedly the best years of our lives at the school. The close relationship one forged with the boys being constantly in and out of the house, with wanting to be fed, or just dropping by for a chat, was something I could never again hope to find in my career.

There were some moments which will remain etched in my memory. Like Himanshu Tyagi, my House Captain, waking me up and telling me in no uncertain terms how upset he was that I had ticked him off in front of the rest of the House. I agonized over this all night and early in the morning before physical training commenced called a 'House Common Room' (meeting) to apologize to the entire house for my act of utter insensitivity. Then there was the evening when from my kitchen (which was separated from the house showers by a very thin wall), I heard some choice abuses being hurled by one Gaurav Bhushan, the school squash champion. I rushed to the showers and gave him a serious mouthful. In response, the next evening at the same time I heard the soulful refrain of *Raghupati Raghav* being sung by a choir of hastily trained juniors, emanating from the showers!

It was not easy for me, therefore, when I received a call for an interview for the position of the Headmaster of the Lawrence School, Lovedale, a position for which I had applied earlier on in the term, with a great deal of encouragement from Shomie Das.

It was the summer of 1991 and term was about to draw to a close. The inter-house hockey Championships were about to commence. Somehow I had a feeling that this would be my last inter-house at Doon School. On the eve of the competition,

I summoned a house meeting.

'Gentlemen,' I said. 'I'm here to ask for a favour. Please win this inter-house, if it's the last thing you do. This is a personal favour I'm asking for and for reasons that I shall disclose later.'

A buzz went around. Had I placed a bet? Could it be that I was leaving? No one was quite sure.

The competition commenced. H house had perhaps the weakest team in the tournament, with virtually no school team players on it. Jaipur House was the favourite. By dint of sheer will power, hard work and more than their fair share of luck, the team actually made it to the final. The final was going to be on the evening when I would be on the bus to Delhi for my interview. I had arranged to stay in Delhi at the home of my house captain, Sawant Pratap Singh—the first time I had allowed myself the privilege of staying in a parents' home. I had arranged with Sawant to phone his father and inform him of the result the moment the game was over. As the bus drew to a stop at Connaught Place, my heart was in my mouth. I knew that Ajay Pratap, Sawant's father, would have the result by them. As I stepped off the bus, a tall, moustachioed man put his arms around me in a bear hug and shouted, 'We've won!'

I heard the full story later. H house had crucified themselves to win the game. They had somehow got a goal in early in the game and hung in there for dear life. Three players had to leave the field injured. But they had done it!

As it happened I got the Lawrence School job and arrived back at Doon School on the morning of the final day of the term. Shomie Das had made the announcement at Assembly. I would be leaving during the summer break. H House seemed devastated. The boys all wandered around with long faces. I was plagued by feelings of guilt. All the elation I had felt at being offered the Lawrence School job seemed to have vanished.

The boys complained bitterly to Indrani, 'Why did you have to do this to us?'

Under the circumstances, I could hardly hope for a farewell. So I decided to organize my own. A tea party was organized in the Common Room. The boys filed in silently. I did the usual homily about what a wonderful innings we had had together. Then one little boy (a C former i.e. class six) got up and choking with tears sobbed, 'This has been a terrible year for us. First Rajiv Gandhi died and now our Housemaster is leaving.'

That summed it all up!

Later on in the night, the mood seemed to have lightened. Groups of boys drifted in and out of the house to chat.

Then someone had an idea, 'Let's "bunk" with DL.'

I was led in a hush-hush fashion to a part of the boundary wall near Jaipur House that had been broken. We scaled the wall and did a pilgrimage to 'Jattis', renowned for its bunandas. Photos were taken. One showed a huge graffiti on the walls of Jattis:

'DL was here!'

15

Off to Lovedale

IF EVER one wants to study how bureaucracy functions in this country, one should visit Shastri Bhavan in New Delhi. After going through the hugely tedious process of getting a pass made to see the person concerned (and heaven help you if that particular officer does not give prior instructions to Reception regarding your appointment), you then proceed through a labyrinth of offices, all of which look depressingly similar, to the office of the bureaucrat you have arranged to meet. When you get to that particular door number, it is more than likely that you will be greeted by a sign saying 'Please meet my PA in Room...'

When you do find that room you enter tentatively and face an army of clerical staff. A couple will be listening to cricket commentary, two others will be engaged in a serious discussion on the price of real estate and a fifth might be at a computer looking busy. Oh yes, there will also be a peon (or two, depending on the rank of the bureaucrat concerned) busy making tea or waiting for the light to turn green (from red), on saheb's door.

'Saheb is in a meeting. You will have to wait.' It never ceases to mystify me how many bureaucrats are in a meeting at any given point of time on any given day.

Finally, if you are lucky on a good day, an hour's wait will see you being ushered into the hallowed chambers, where from behind a mountain of files you can spot "God" himself. The rooms, particularly those of the senior officers, are huge and I suppose deliberately designed to make you feel particularly small. The bureaucrat will extend a cursory greeting and ask you to take a seat on the cumbrous office sofa. It would be interesting to do a study on how much of the taxpayers' money is spent on decorating bureaucrats offices all over the country.

It was in one such office in Shastri Bhavan that I found myself being ushered into for an audience with the Secretary, Education, Government of India, on a May morning in 1991. Little did I know at the time what a great role this office was to play in my life for many years to come. The interview board to select the headmaster of the Lawrence School, Lovedale, had assembled in the office of the Secretary, Education. The Secretary himself, Mr Anil Bordia, struck me immediately as someone as far removed from the stereotypical bureaucrat as one could imagine. Warm and welcoming, yet direct and to the point.

When everyone on the Board had exhausted their list of questions for me, Mr Bordia turned around and said,' Young man, let me be very honest. Although I am the Chairman, I would not wish this school in its present state on my worst enemy. You may just find it too hot to handle. This being your first Headship, it can either make or break you.' He then went on to suggest that he could arrange for a lien of six months on my services with Doon School. If in these six months, I found Lawrence School difficult, I would have the option of rejoining Doon School.

It did not take me more than a few seconds to reject this idea. After all, if I were to take up the assignment knowing that I had a soft option, I was already condemning myself to failure. I would have to go in both feet first and deal with whatever was in store for me. I signed a typical government order appointing me headmaster of Lawrence School. It was obvious that the school was not very high on the ministry's priorities, as apart from my salary the order said nothing about my duties and responsibilities. Armed with a copy I walked out of the Secretary's office to begin a new chapter in our lives.

16

Beneath the Beauty

ALL WHO have seen the Lawrence School, Lovedale, will know of its stunning beauty. Situated in the Nilgiris at a height of nearly seven thousand feet the campus sprawls over approximately seven hundred acres of hill and dale, most of it forest. These landscapes are home to an incredible variety of plant and animal life. Very few schools in the world can boast of such an amazing campus.

'Do not get taken in by its beauty,' warned an ex-head girl of the school who happened to be a friend in Dehradun. 'These are very troubled times for the school and there are sinister currents running underneath.'

Founded in 1858 by Sir Henry Lawrence, the school was originally home to the children of British soldiers orphaned during the great revolt of 1857. Later it opened up its doors to Anglo Indians and finally to Indians. Created in a military mould, the school took great pride in its military traditions. The students wore battledress to class, the Founders Day was known for its spectacular march past and the beating of the retreat (there were three bands in the school), and the Prefectorial body wore epaulettes distinguishing themselves from the others.

In the midst of all this martial ardour, a very sickening

tradition, masquerading as part of the military ethos, had crept in. That was bullying. The seniors thought it their God-given right to hit juniors with hockey sticks at the slightest excuse, so much so that bones were broken on a fairly regular basis. The worst sufferers were the students of class nine which was the junior-most class in Senior school (classes nine to twelve). In the Middle school (classes seven and eight), students of class eight bullied those of class seven. The Prep School (classes four to six) was not afflicted by this tradition, and neither was the Girl's School (the boarding where all the girls resided).

As a matter of fact, one of the more endearing aspects of the school was that it was co-educational. The girls were, by far and large, charming, sophisticated and poised and added a touch of class to the school. They were also very good at their studies and at sports. They were indeed a great ally to have in my future efforts to improve the atmosphere of the school.

Amongst the boys there was a codified system of favours by which the seniors could ask a junior to do anything for them at any time. Each class twelve student had a 'Piza'. This was a title sanctified by tradition denoting the equivalent of a personal slave. I came across Pizas sneaking across the campus in the dead of the night to fetch clothes for their masters from the dhobi-ghat which was located at one end of the campus. Often Pizas had to sit by the bed of their master to wake him up at an appointed hour. Failure to live up to the senior's expectations invited serious retribution. There was at least one case of a boy being branded with an electric iron!

One particular incident will haunt me to the day I die. I was about three months into my tenure when one morning, an enraged mother of a class seven boy stormed into my office. She took off her son's shirt and showed me the huge red welts on his back. The boy had been systematically thrashed in the night by the boys of class eight with wet towels. His fault? He had dared to defeat a boy from the class above in the finals of a prestigious school tennis tournament called the 'Rob Roy' tournament, ironically sponsored by a well-known alumnus.

The mother's words still ring in my ears, 'I may be able to cure the scars on his back but what about the scars on his soul?'

As I started to spend time with the boys, I realized that they were not the savage vicious creatures one might expect them to be, especially in view of the horrific incidents of bullying that the campus kept witnessing. On the contrary they were courteous, well-mannered and all from very respectable families. There was obviously something seriously wrong with the environment they were in. This observation started giving me some insights into how to tackle the bullying problem.

It is my view that not only is bullying completely morally reprehensible, it also creates an atmosphere of fear that stifles creativity. Not only are the victims often scarred for life, but whilst at school they are unable to achieve their potential as they spend the better part of their best years cowering in fear. In my view, as the Head of school, I owed it to every child entrusted to my care to provide a level playing field so that all could grow and explore their talents and strengths with a sense of joy and abandon.

Bullying was not the only problem staring me in the face. One of the problems that plagues our education system in general and the public school system in particular, is the woeful shortage of good teachers. It is a sad fact that most of those who opt for teaching, particularly in remote boarding schools, rarely do so as a first choice. The head of the school very rarely has the privilege of being able to choose from a large catchment area of trained teachers, in the same manner that a corporate head does in terms of his personnel requirements.

Whilst Lawrence School was singularly blessed in some of the teachers that it had, it too shared the problem endemic to most residential schools. The fact that this body was seriously fractured only added to my woes. Some suggested that it was a Tamil vs Malayalee problem. Being from north of the Vindhyas I was blissfully unaware of this divide, which was just as well because it allowed me to ignore these divisions even if they did exist. The better teachers in the faculty seemed to have been thoroughly deflated by the indiscipline that prevailed in the school. Most felt threatened by the senior boys and with good reason. Private property such as scooters and cars were frequently vandalized, particularly if a teacher reported an act of indiscipline to the authorities.

Then there was a problem of a near complete breakdown of administrative procedures. Almost as soon as I had taken over, the District Forest Officer (DFO), called me up to inform me that someone involved in School security was selling timber from the school forest. The kitchen staff could load as much food as they wanted in their 'tiffin carriers' and take it home. This resulted in them cooking much more than what was required for any given meal. All that was left over was theirs for the taking! Every single department suffered from some such serious infirmity.

The infrastructure was in shambles. The school went

without electricity for days at a stretch particularly during the monsoons as there was no generator backup. The toilet for the senior boys called 'Big Bogs' was my idea of what hell must be like. One visit there was enough to make me want to throw up. The gymnasium was a shell of a building with virtually no equipment. There were no decent tennis courts. The list was endless and to my mind all this was a backdrop to the atmosphere of indiscipline that prevailed in the school.

A very fundamental problem with our educational system is that there is no training for heads of schools. A B.Ed or M.Ed can never prepare you for the challenges of Headship. It is testimony to the low priority given to school education, that there is no institution with the brand equity of, say, the IIM's to impart training to Heads. And yet Heads have a task far more daunting then many corporate managers do. And here I was, a young Headmaster straight out of Doon School, expected to tackle this hydra headed monster!

17

Into the Fray

There was nothing left to it except to roll up one's sleeves and get down to it. The discipline of the school was obviously the first priority. And it was clear that it could not be treated just as a law and order problem. There had to be a change in the mindset and for that the trust deficit had to be eliminated as quickly and as far as possible. I had no illusions about the Herculean nature of the task ahead.

I quickly realized that I needed professional help. With the help of a parent I enlisted the services of the Promise Foundation in Bangalore. Gideon Arulmani and his wife Sonali, travelled up to Lawrence School each month to conduct counselling programs. Sonali has since gone on to become a fellow of the Royal College of Sciences in the UK and has a chair at Oxford and Gideon is a consultant to the United Nations on issues involving child abuse and welfare. I like to think that the Lawrence School experience provided them the platform for this huge quantum leap.

Gideon and Sonali gave me some great insights into the problem of bullying. Bullying thrives in an atmosphere of fear and lack of trust in the authorities. A combination of these two factors means that victims never speak up as they fear they will be let down by the authorities and persecuted by their seniors. So there is an 'omerta' or conspiracy of silence.

As far as the perpetrators are concerned, the battle lies in convincing them that bullying is not macho. Rather it is an act of cowardice. The Prefects had to be convinced that real authority comes from being role models, not from instilling fear.

One of the first things that we did was to get the entire Prefectorial body together and work out the ground rules. 'If we do not give physical punishment, how are we going to be effective?' they asked. This was an argument that I was to hear time and time again and not only at Lawrence School.

In consultation with the Prefect body an elaborate structure of punishment and rewards (minus physical punishment), involving a system of cards (much like in football) for different degrees of offences was worked out. A disciplinary committee was created with housemasters and prefects finding representation on it. Any serious offence was to be scrutinized by the committee and the offender too received a fair hearing. The committee had to be unanimous in their decision, no matter how long it took. The biggest challenge, as I discovered, was to persuade the students on the committee that they were there as jury and not as lawyers for the defence. I am very pleased to say that over the years the students warmed to the task and indeed provided us, the faculty, with interesting perspectives on various issues. It was a great learning experience for me. There were of course times when harsh methods including expulsion had to be adopted. But such measures were taken only in the case of repeat offenders and always with the approval of the Disciplinary Committee.

One of the biggest lessons I learnt very early on was that the disciplinary norms, no matter how stringent, would be accepted by the student body as long as they a) had been consulted in framing them, b) were implemented consistently and c) were fair in their application. No one, no matter how influential the parents, would be shown any preferential treatment. We made these principles the linchpin of our system.

The tutorial system, whereby each teacher had a group of students for whom he/she was directly responsible, was created. All attempts were made to revive the 'House Spirit' and to promote a healthy inter-house rivalry. The seniors were encouraged to coach the juniors, whether it be sports, debate or any co-curricular activity. There was also a system of academic tutorials, where seniors were made responsible for tutoring juniors who were struggling academically. They were also encouraged to take the juniors on a 'guided tour' of the senior dormitories, so that the juniors did not imagine senior school to be a horrible monster's lair, where these creatures were lying in wait to gobble them up!

All this was great in principle but in practice it was a different matter. There were repeated violations. And I must confess that there were times when these violations got the better of me. I know that a few times when in spite of my repeated entreaties (with folded hands on some occasions), or threats, or counselling, a little boy would be brought into my presence, bleeding profusely because he had either been whipped with a rifle butt, or with a belt, or even branded with an electric iron, I occasionally took the extreme step of administering some fairly tight slaps or even a few of the best with a cane to the offender. The senseless and sickening violence frustrated me immensely. A sustained campaign of counselling was introduced, overseen by Gideon and Sonali.

In spite of all these efforts, it seemed to me sometimes that for every step forward that we took, we ended up taking two steps backwards. But I was determined not to give in. There were times when the formal structures had to be abandoned. I remember doing the rounds one night and coming across one of the boys lying dead drunk in the infamous 'Big Bogs'. Earlier that week he had learnt that his father had committed suicide. I picked him up and carried him to the dormitory. In the process he threw up (and most of it over me) and I had to clean him up and put him to bed. The next day I summoned him to my office. He was quaking with fear. I assured him that whatever happened the night before was a matter between the two of us and would remain so. I asked him how he felt.

'Awful,' he replied.

'And did drinking help with the problem you were facing?'

'No sir.'

'Well then, there's your lesson. All you've got out of this is a massive hangover. Certainly not worth it is it?'

'No sir.'

With that the meeting concluded. I never had trouble with the young man again.

The fact that we were indeed moving in the right direction as far as eliminating bullying was concerned was driven home to me on April Fool's day, about two years into my headship of the school. That evening, while I was having a farewell cup of tea with one of the graduating students, the doorbell rang and a dishevelled little boy from class nine with a seemingly bloodied nose frantically begged me to accompany him to the dormitories as the seniors were reportedly on the rampage with their hockey sticks. As was to be expected my blood pressure started doing cartwheels and I ran off after the little boy to the dormitory in question. As I entered the dormitory, I noticed that it was in complete darkness. I was shocked to see that the House Captain was one of my most trusted students, so I shouted (in a very Shakespearean manner, I may add), 'Even you, Machiah?' Just then, as if on cue, the lights came on and the entire dormitory burst into a chorus, 'April Fool, Sir!' The fact that the monster of bullying could be treated as an April Fool's joke, perhaps told its own story.

Some wonderful relationships with the students developed along the way. I remember a young boy and his sister being delivered to my house with police escort and a lawyer, because the parents were involved in a bitter wrangle and threats of kidnapping had been issued. The court had ruled that the children were to stay with the Headmaster during the vacation! For Indrani and me it was a great opportunity to befriend these two children and be of some help to them during these traumatic times. Some years later the boy had to appear in court to depose against his own father. As soon as he stepped out of the court he called me and informed me that during the hearing he had just lost his cool and slapped his father! It was obviously very important to him to know what my reaction was. All I could say was that such an action was not the solution to the problem and at some stage he might wish to consider an apology. It was a big learning experience for me as well.

But it was not always that easy, particularly when the parents got involved and issued dire threats. I remember getting a call from the Prime Minister's Office asking me to reinstate a boy who had been expelled for indiscipline. I was told by the senior officer on the phone that the father of the boy was very close to the Prime Minister and that it was the Prime Minister's personal request. I politely refused, saying that I could not compromise the discipline of the school and certainly not when an entire committee had taken the decision. The gentleman on the line then asked me if I knew what the consequences of my refusal could be. I replied that I was fully aware that I might be in serious trouble with the Prime Minister. The phone went dead. Much to my surprise, I never heard anything on the subject, until a few years later when I was attending a get-together of alumni and an old student walked up to me and reminded me of that telephone call. He was actually the older brother of the boy in question and he said, 'Sir, though I was party to that call being made, I would have lost all respect for my old school had you given in.'

A very strange way of receiving a compliment indeed!

Along with fighting negative influences, the attempt was to build on the positives. A system of 'Open House' was introduced, whereby on a monthly basis each class would elect two representatives and send them armed with complaints and suggestions for the improvement of the school. The meeting would be held in my house and senior faculty would be present. Minutes were kept and follow up action initiated. Any issue relating to the welfare of the school was welcome. Many interesting initiatives resulted, including an 'Official Dating Time' on Sundays!

Any new rule that we wished to introduce in school was thoroughly discussed and debated in this forum, sometimes for weeks. The understanding was that once there was an acceptance of a rule, there was automatically a consensus on the consequence that would result as an infringement of that rule.

A turning point of sorts occurred in my life as an educator, when I attended a seminar entitled 'Raising standards of pupil achievement through the training and development of Headteachers and principals of schools' organized by the British Council at Chichester in the United Kingdom, in July 1999.

On arrival at the seminar, I was slightly nonplussed to see that the only other Indian there was a government veterinarian from Pantnagar! When I asked him what he was doing there he sheepishly explained that someone in the bureaucracy had made an enormous gaffe and he had been deputed to the wrong seminar! Anyway the gentleman was not too put out as he got a free trip abroad as a consequence.

At the seminar also was a Pakistani head of school, who actually occupied the room next to me and we became good friends. This was incidentally the time of the Kargil war and both of us would scan the news anxiously each day. When we went for our walks in the evening all we did was bemoan the fate of our respective countries, and the fact that all that we were offering the children of the next generation was a future full of hatred and animosity. It is interesting in hindsight to reflect on our reactions when both of us were far removed from all the jingoism and chest-thumping surrounding the event.

The seminar itself was a mind-blowing professional experience. For the first time I realized how much I needed to learn about Headship and about how far behind we were as a country in our vision regarding good schools and progressive educational practices.

On my return to Lovedale, I shared my experience with my colleagues at a 'mini-seminar' and started putting into practice some of what I considered to be more effective lessons that I had learnt there. Thus teacher appraisals (including the appraisal of the Headmaster by senior faculty and students), teamwork between departments to encourage integrated learning, a greater emphasis on research and reference – all started to gradually find their place in the school's scheme of things. In retrospect, my disillusionment with some of the traditions of the school, which I felt were holding the school in 'medieval' shackles also began here. This plus the fact that a number of the faculty were really upset with some of the changes (particularly those demanding greater accountability) perhaps laid the foundation for a great deal of the troubles that I was to face later.

It was, and is, my considered belief, that schools in India spend too much time looking at themselves. It's all about better board exam results than the others, winning all the inter-school tournaments and other such accomplishments. While all these are certainly important, it is equally important, I feel, to teach children empathy, especially for those not as privileged as themselves. Schools, in my view, must produce citizens who will not only have a burning desire to excel in whatever they do but also want to make a difference to the society around them. I tried very hard to make this our credo in Lawrence.

Several initiatives were therefore launched. One of these was street theatre by which we helped the children in the surrounding villages perform to drive home messages against alcoholism and wife and child abuse. I will never forget the time one of the villagers (known for his alcoholism) came to my office to tell me about the moment of truth he experienced when he saw his own son performing in the street theatre in his village (the play had been directed by students) and acting out the role of his father (i.e. him).

'I saw myself for the first time as the monster that I become every evening,' the father sobbed in my office. 'I swear never to touch alcohol again,' he added.

To keep the young men working in the nearby tea estates from hitting the bottle each evening after work, I persuaded the students to organize a football tournament for all the youth in that area. The tea companies rose marvellously to the occasion and gave generous sponsorships. Consequently, all the villages around Lawrence School were abuzz with football fever for most of the year, busy preparing for the big tournament. This kept all the youth happily engaged in a healthy pursuit; at the end of it there was this hugely popular tournament conducted almost entirely by the senior boys at Lawrence School. I like to think the boys learnt lessons no classroom could have taught.

Values such as integrity and honesty cannot be taught except by example. And often the lesson is a hard one. One such opportunity came my way in the form of an inter-school athletics championship. The Lawrence School had for many years lost its pre-eminent position in the inter-school athletics championships held each year at Wellington, the army base near Conoor. The reason for this was primarily that the competition was held soon after Lawrence School reopened after the monsoon break, leaving our athletes very little time to train and get fit for the event.

One year a member of the Board and an alumnus, T. Gundan, announced that he would give a prize of one lakh rupees to the athletics team if they could win that year. Coming in the wake of the great urging by the Department of Physical Education, this was all that the students needed. The athletes reported back to school in the middle of the monsoon break for a training camp. And bless their little hearts, they toiled for hours in the rain to get fit and hone their skills.

When the time came for the championship (spread out over three days), Lawrence School shot into the lead on the very first day. The lead had become very impressive on the second day, but in the evening I found a rather long-faced Department of Physical Education shuffle into my drawing room to seek a meeting. What had transpired was that towards the end of the second day's events, it had been discovered by the officials that one of our girls, who had actually bagged a large number of points for us, should actually have been competing in a section above the one she was entered in on account of a mistake in entering her date of birth. I asked the Department whether indeed it was a genuine mistake and they assured me that it was. I quickly put their fears at rest and promised them that I would speak to the jury and request them to allow the girl compete in a higher section the next day and in the meantime strike off all the points that she had so far earned for us. Even so, we were comfortably in the lead.

That night, before I actually made the call, I decided to check the records for myself. To my horror, I discovered that the girl's actual date of birth had been fudged in the records. The next morning, I went straight to the bus in which the athletes were proceeding to the competition and asked them how many actually knew the truth. Reluctantly, most hands went up. I asked the athletes to get off the bus and informed them that we were no longer participating in the competition.

'Why Sir,' asked the athletics captain, 'are you punishing all of us when only one is responsible?'

'Sorry son,' I replied, 'all of you are responsible. All of you knew the truth but everyone kept your mouths shut. When something wrong is being done you must learn to take a stand. Otherwise you are as guilty as the actual offender.'

The incident kicked up quite a storm. Many of the alumni were up in arms for the same reason that the athletics captain had been upset. The media too had a field day. Why should the whole squad suffer an account of one person? I was asked this question repeatedly. I was, however, and still remain convinced that it was the appropriate thing to do.

The struggle for infrastructure was an equally uphill one. Early on, I realized that school morale was very low on account of the poor infrastructure. And the long days without electricity were the worst culprit. A quick trip to Chennai for a meeting with the Secretary, Power ensured that we were shifted from the rural to the high-tension line. Of course some deft fundraising was necessary and since I was new to all this, I found myself escaping from the electrical contractor through the back door of the office as I had not been able to muster the payment for his bills. However, as time went by I became better at this exercise and did not have to face embarrassment again.

Then a look at the alumni records revealed a very vital name; Kirloskar. This time a trip to Bangalore and Vikram Kirloskar himself very generously donated a massive generator to the school. It was a matter of time before help poured in from stalwarts and well-wishers like Krishna Kumar of Tatas, Philip Mathew of the Malayalam Manorama, Narayan Rao of NDTV, ML Alagappan of the Murugappa Group. Other helpful alumni such as Jose Dominic, one of the country's leading hoteliers, Theo Devagnanyam of Needle industries, Johnny Paul of Popular Motors and other leading scions of industry generously contributed. This allowed us to be able to redo all the toilets (including Big Bogs). We built new staff quarters, tennis courts and a swimming pool, added six new vehicles to the school's old fleet of three, developed a four hundred metre running track (perhaps the first of its kind at that altitude), equipped the shell of a gymnasium with state-of-the-art exercise machines, built a new horse-riding arena and outfitted the classrooms with modern furniture and IT facilities. All this greatly helped in reducing the trust deficit.

The academic front had to be revitalized. Staff morale had to be addressed. The Board fortunately saw this clearly and sanctioned some impressive salary hikes.

There was a very interesting incident in connection with salary hikes. The kitchen staff had become used to cooking much more than the required amounts and carting the rest off home. On one occasion after I had negotiated a hefty pay rise for all the employees (which was to be kept secret till Founders day that year) I ordered a ban on any food carried out of the kitchen. Security staff were instructed to body frisk if necessary. As it happened, on the eve of Founders day, Madhavan, the head cook (who was also the unsanctioned leader of the unofficial workers union), was frisked just outside the gates of my residence. He objected violently and in full view of all proceeded to strip stark naked. The matter was brought to my notice and I gave instructions that Madhavan be brought inside my residence. I was, at the time, laid up in bed with a fresh pacemaker implant.

There behind closed doors I calmly confronted a violently shaking Madhavan and informed him that I had planned to announce a mighty pay hike the next day, but in view of the fact then the unofficial union leader preferred to take food home instead, I would call off the hike and inform all the staff that they could carry on taking the extra food home but there would not be an increase of even a rupee in salary. The entire blame would be laid at Madhavan's door. Madhavan's bravado disappeared instantly. He virtually fell on his knees and begged forgiveness.

'Dorai (master),' he pleaded, 'my colleagues will hang me if this happens.' Thus we prevented what could have been a potentially embarrassing situation and perhaps even a full-blown strike.

It was perhaps an irony of fate that some years later Madhavan was diagnosed with terminal cancer. I appealed to the whole school and all rose manfully to the occasion. Between all of us, students and faculty, we were able to raise five lakh rupees for Madhavan's treatment and he was flown out to the Tata Cancer Hospital in Mumbai. The doctors managed to give him a five-year extension on his life. It was one of the most fulfilling things I have ever done.

The teaching faculty needed more than just money. They needed a sense of pride in what they were doing and regular training to become more professional. Training programmes and workshops became the order of the day. The Science faculty, as a matter of fact, as a result of a series of workshops with Samar Bagchi (the brain behind the famous TV show called Quest), authored a series of textbooks that were published by the OUP. We pioneered, I believe, at least in the public school system, the first Assisted Learning Department, devoted exclusively to children with learning difficulties such as dyslexia and this was long before Aamir Khan came up with the film 'Taare Zameen Par'.

The faculty club was outfitted with a new television and a billiards table and faculty get-togethers were encouraged. As a matter of fact, the tables used to be cleared after a faculty dinner and the faculty would do 'Bhangra' that would put the lads and the lasses of Punjab to shame!

One of the problems I noticed at Lawrence was the big gap between the teachers and taught. This was quite unlike Doon School where there was an easy camaraderie between the two, fostered greatly by mid-term treks, playing sports together and other informal gatherings. In Lawrence, on the other hand, the relationships were quite formal. In an attempt to bridge this gap, I initiated a program on Childrens' Day when the teachers would get on the stage and perform a number of spoofs on the students. It was all in good humour and the students rocked with laughter seeing their teachers dressed up like them and pulling out all the skeletons from the closet, ones which they thought had been carefully concealed. The added advantage was that the teachers learnt not to take themselves too seriously!

Of course, the students had their go at us on Teachers' Day (which preceded Childrens' Day), by doing a similar spoof. They were allowed to imitate the teachers provided they imitated the Headmaster first and the imitation was not personally offensive. I am proud to say that in all my years at Lovedale this code was never violated, as indeed at Welham Boys' School which I later headed and where I initiated this practice.

The nine years or so that I spent at Lovedale also gave me a great opportunity to befriend and be befriended by some great characters in the Nilgiris. Siasp Kothavalah, a retired but legendary planter and Doon School alumnus, who ran a wonderful lodge called Bamboo Banks on the edge of the Mudumulai reserve, became a great friend. Indrani and I would head off to spend a weekend with him and his gracious wife Zarine whenever the pressure got to us. Similarly, another planter and naturalist, 'Bertie' Suarez, and his charming wife Jenny provided a welcome getaway from the demanding task of running the school. 'Bertie' was unfortunately taken away from our midst in a most tragic accident when he was trying to rescue a bison that had fallen into a pit. It was ironic that the jungle that Bertie loved so much took him away as well.

If indeed, I experienced any success at Lovedale and even later, it was largely on account of Indrani. Not only was she an excellent teacher, but she took on the onerous responsibility of being a hostess and a charming and gracious one at that.

In the schools of the nature of the ones I headed, this was no mean feat. There was never a weekend when the house was not inundated with guests or students. Indrani looked after all of them, according the same warmth and welcome to the students as to the members of the Board. The faculty and students soon came to trust her with their secrets. As for me, I could not have asked for a better sounding board for all my plans and ideas. It was only when I did not heed her advice that I had to pay a price.

It was all too easy in the tumult generated by the efforts to rebuild Lawrence School, to forget that I had a young family growing up in the same house. I am afraid that, to a large extent, I did. Diya and Shama were indeed soaking in all that the school had to offer. In the chaos of each day and the challenges that seemed to come my way, it was very difficult to squeeze in quality time with them. Of course, we rode together each day, but then there were thirty others with us at the same time and all quite focused on the lesson of the day. I did gather from snatches of their conversation that being the Head's daughters was not always easy for them. They were given a hard time (as was to be expected) for some of the unpopular decisions that I had to take.

But just how difficult it was, was brought home to me by one particular incident. Indrani and I had been away for a conference and during our absence Diya happened to have an argument with a classmate. The boy, in a fit of anger, slapped her hard and sent her sprawling to the floor. The Deputy Headmaster, who was officiating in my absence, immediately suspended the boy. The fallout was devastating for Diya. She was boycotted by almost the entire school, including the girls. The daughter who we met on return was shaking tearful, and a bundle of nerves. It was, needless to say, a difficult moment for me, being torn between being a Headmaster and a father. I immediately reinstated the boy, called an assembly of the entire school and pleaded with them as a father to take my daughter back into the fold. That was the only time that I have regretted being a Head of school and I daresay, that without the family's support nothing would have been possible.

No account of Lovedale would be complete without a perspective on what was, funnily enough, to become the most emotive issue in the community; horse riding.

The Lawrence School, Lovedale was one of the few schools in the country at the time to offer horse riding as part of its sports curriculum. This really excited me as I was fond of horses. My father's retirement from the army unfortunately cut short whatever little opportunity I had to indulge in the sport. My experience of the sport had taught me that horse riding was great for developing confidence and compassion in young people. To discover that Lawrence had a riding program was thus hugely encouraging.

Imagine my horror when I discovered that the so-called riding establishment consisted of four retired army horses, virtually dying of starvation and afflicted by lameness (one actually died chewing asbestos in sheer desperation). I had two choices—either to close down the establishment, or start afresh. Given the way I felt about the sport, it was a no-brainer. With no funds, I used money from my precious Provident Fund to secure three retired race horses from the Ooty race course.

That was the beginning of a long saga. It would perhaps take a book by itself to relate the story of the equestrian establishment of Lawrence School. It involved travelling to racecourses around, such as Bangalore and Chennai, spotting good prospects, persuading owners and trainers to donate these to the school and then retraining them for riding, including sports such as show jumping, dressage and cross-country. Huge funding was required and at a time when the battle to improve infrastructure was in full swing, no school funds could naturally be diverted for the purpose.

Help arrived in the form of Five Stars Shipping. Based in Mumbai, the firm was owned by KN Dhunjibhoy, who I was introduced to by an alumnus of the school, Adil Ghandy. To this day KN Dhunjibhoy owns some of the finest racehorses in the country. I flew to Mumbai and did a presentation for him. Within half an hour he had committed an amount of three lakh rupees a year to the school. When I asked him what he expected in return, he just smiled and said, 'Keep producing champions.'

As our team went on excelling itself and winning one championship after another he kept stepping up the donation, until it touched twelve lakh rupees the year I left Lawrence School (2000). Thanks to the subsidy, the riding fee could be kept down to a ridiculous two hundred rupees a month and at least two hundred and fifty students rode voluntarily.

More importantly perhaps, our success in fighting all odds and winning these laurels inspired many other riding clubs and schools, particularly in the south of India and I am told that today equestrian sport has become virtually a movement. We also invited the children from the local school for challenged children for riding lessons which our students imparted. I like to think that the lives of both parties were immeasurably richer as a result.

But there was another perspective on this issue. 'Lawrence has been reduced to a riding school' was the oft-heard refrain from a section of the community, particularly the alumni. The fact that the newspapers were often full of our successful exploits in riding competitions across the country only added grist to the mill.

In retrospect, I can see now how my personal involvement in the sport would have encouraged such a perspective. One year I actually won a bronze at the national championships and it is perhaps a dubious distinction that I am perhaps the first person with a pacemaker to have done so! Although I had taken official leave to which I was entitled, for the event, the buzz was that the headmaster went riding much like Nero fiddling whilst Rome burnt!

This perception (call it criticism, if you may), was often taken to absurd limits. When Khusroo Dhunjibhoy, thoroughly impressed with our consistent success, made an offer to set up a world class equestrian training facility at Lovedale at a cost of over Rs. 1 crore (no mean figure in those days), the Memorandum of Understanding (MOU) that was drawn up by the school lawyer gave the school virtual proprietary rights over the venture. The Board very enthusiastically agreed, but on the virtual eve of the meeting scheduled to sign the MOU, backed out. It seems that a powerful section of the alumni felt that the sport was too closely linked to me as an individual and the school should therefore steer clear of it. I am still to fathom the logic was behind this line of thinking.

As a matter of fact, I was also engaging with an international sports good manufacturer to develop a high altitude training centre for Indian athletes at the school. But once the Board backed out of the negotiations for the equestrian centre, I could not bring myself to go down that road again.

As our success grew, so did the criticism. Whilst I fully understand where my critics came from, I can say with all honesty that I did not let any other aspect of the school suffer on account of riding. What my critics also failed to understand was that the sport created a huge bonding between the students and me. All of two hundred and fifty students rode regularly and I rode with them. On horseback we were all equal. We were as vulnerable as each other, we loved the animals and cared for them together, we took instruction together and this created a very strong link between the students and me. Every winter Indrani and I escorted the riding team with our horses to the national championships. We lived in the same dorm, ate the same food and lived and breathed the successes and failures together. I will never forget one bitter winter in Delhi when we all lived together under tents in the freezing cold and ate the same langar food served by the army. I cannot think of a better way to bond with one's students.

Perhaps one of the defining moments associated with the sport was provided when we opened it up to the children from the school for the challenged, which was in Ooty. Twice a week a busload of them would arrive and it was a joy to see our young riders proudly take charge of their 'wards' and instruct them in the art of horse riding. As a matter of fact, on one Founder's Day, these special children even participated in the Equestrian display. As one of the girl riders from Lawrence put it, 'The first time we put these kids on a horse, they were screaming in fear. Now they scream when we try and take them off!'

Moreover, the sport had a huge positive impact on those students who were, on account of a lack of self confidence or self esteem, not doing as well as their peers either in the classroom or in other areas of school life. One remarkable case was that of a little girl who had not secured entry into any other school as she 'flunked' every entrance examination she took.

And she failed because she was highly dyslexic. Consequently, she was not very keen on being carted off to any new school.

The parents had heard that we took a very sympathetic view of such problems and were indeed equipped to deal with them and so they brought her to Lawrence in the hope of securing admission. It was a surly little girl who accompanied us on a tour of the school, till such time as we went past the paddocks where the horses were grazing. Her face lit up and she ran to one of the horses and started petting it. 'Papa, can I join this school?' she asked excitedly. Not only did she join, but she went on to become a superb rider and an excellent student. The sport while open to criticism, suddenly had a lot to recommend it.

The horses also provided some unique teaching and learning moments. One year we had to load our horses on to the train at Madras railway station to take them all the way to Shillong for the Junior National Championships. As was our practice, the entire team participated in this loading exercise and it was not left just to the grooms. Each rider was responsible for his/her horse.

When we arrived at the station, the authorities pointed us to a deserted railway platform at the end of which the wagon that we had booked for the horses was waiting. We were informed that there was still time for the train to arrive and that we should get our horses on as quickly as possible. The authorities ought to have told the horses as well, for just on that day the beasts decided not to cooperate in getting off from the trucks that had carried them to the railway station. And sure enough by the time they did get off, the train had arrived and the platform was chaotic with people trying to get on the train.

We were on the horns of a dilemma. We could call off the exercise, in which case we might never make it to the competition, or we could try and load our skittish thoroughbreds while negotiating the madness in front. The only problem was that if one horse panicked the other eleven would follow and we would have a stampede and a possible bloodbath on our hands. The team looked at me for an answer. I asked for my horse, 'Brown Saheb', and led him forward, signalling to the others to follow in single file. I knew that if my horse could keep calm the others would as well. That one hundred yard stretch was longer than any marathon that I have run. I kept whispering endearments into my horse's ear whilst helping him negotiate the swirling crowds and loud noises that appeared like a deluge around us. In about fifteen minutes we were all safely on. I collapsed on the dry hay in the wagon, reduced to a pool of sweat.

This was not a lesson in leadership that I could have picked up from any management institute or from some book on leadership available at a railway or airport book stall. But it was indeed a lesson that would stand me in good stead all my life and perhaps it has helped some of the students who were there on the day. But perceptions are difficult to change, as I discovered, and little did I know at the time what a heavy price I would have to pay for this particular one.

18

Matters of the Heart

Ever since I was rushed off to the Doon Hospital, I had not experienced similar health ailments. With doctors not being sure if the episode was related to the heart, I had continued with my running. At Lovedale, running through the forests and over hill and dale was an different experience and I revelled in it. I also enjoyed the distinction of winning the school cross country race, three years on the trot. It was customary for me to do a ten kilometre run every morning. It cleared my head and gave me an opportunity to reflect on various issues at hand. One such May morning in 1993, with Founder's Day looming on the horizon, I returned from my run to find that for some inexplicable reason, I was feeling utterly exhausted, enough to not to be able to brush my teeth. I telephoned the school doctor who opined that we go as soon as possible to a cardiologist at Ooty. As I had scheduled an important meeting with some of my colleagues regarding the upcoming Founder's Day in the morning, I requested her to hold on to the travel plans for a while.

Unfortunately, the meeting took more time than anticipated. However, Dr Jyotsna Sharan, the school doctor, would brook no delay. She stormed into my office and announced, 'Ladies and gentlemen, this meeting is adjourned.

I am taking the Headmaster to the hospital.' With that she bundled me and Indrani, who was returning after finishing her classes, into the car.

At the nursing home I was quickly plugged into an ECG machine. As the machine began spewing out the paper, I saw a look of horror on the cardiologist's face. Before I had time to ask whether he was feeling unwell, he virtually vaulted over me, grabbed a medical device and banged it on my chest. The resultant shock made me scream in pain and I passed out. That was my introduction to the world of defibrillators and sadly they are now an integral part of my life, so much so, that I am implanted with one in my abdomen! Once again I went through a round of tests. I was taken to the Apollo Hospital in Madras, where they declared that I suffered from 'Sick Sinus Syndrome' which resulted in irregular heartbeats. The answer apparently was to implant a pacemaker

Armed with a pacemaker, I returned to Lovedale. Running was ruled out so I started to ride with a vengeance. The students were so much better than me, including my own daughters, and I had a lot of catching up to do. The pacemaker sadly did not seem to solve my problem. One day, when walking up a Lovedale slope, I collapsed. Medical opinion was of the view that I should go for some electrophysiological tests. Dr Som Raju and Dr Ravi Kishore, both eminent electro-physiologists, worked at Medicity in Hyderabad. Indrani and I made the trip to Medicity, where after running numerous tests, the doctors put me on beta-blockers.

All this seemed to be going well, until 1998. That year, the Equestrian Federation of India decided to host an international equestrian championship in Bangalore and I was asked to organize it. This meant that I had to shift to Bangalore during the school winter vacation of that year. The pressure of organizing such a major event was understandably enormous. As I sat in the school riding instructor's tent on the last day of the event, while one of our Lovedale students went on to win gold, I experienced an acute feeling of nausea. Naib Risaldar Pale Ram, the riding instructor, was quick to realize that something was seriously wrong. He summoned the ambulance parked at the event and directed that I be taken to the nearest hospital.

As the ambulance sped through the streets, I had a sinking feeling that my life was slowly draining out of me. I could just feel my life going through my abdomen and down to my toes. The paramedic kept shouting in my ear, 'Mr Lahiri, don't go to sleep! We are almost there!' As the doctors at the emergency hovered over me, I screamed, 'Doc I am going, save me!' The doctor in turn went straight for the defibrillator. One huge shock and then the bliss of unconsciousness...

Indrani, who had been with me in Bangalore, had only just returned to Lovedale when she received a phone call informing her that I was in the hospital. She asked the driver to turn around and drive her back to Bangalore. An alumnus of the school, Keith Butler, who happened to be visiting from Australia, very kindly accompanied her. She arrived in the early hours of the morning just as I was coming back into consciousness. I am told that my words to her were, 'Well!' now we know that I definitely have a heart problem!'

Whilst I was in the intensive care unit at the hospital, Indrani came to know through the relatives of another patient there that Dr Ravi Kishore had moved from Hyderabad to Bangalore and was at the Manipal hospital, working with the famous Dr Devi

Shetty. A few telephone calls later, Dr Ravi Kishore had arranged for me to be transferred to Manipal to be under his care.

At Manipal, serious investigations (which included simulating the same symptoms that I had felt earlier, under controlled conditions) were conducted. After one such session, when I was recovering from being defibbed, Dr Ravi Kishore excitedly approached me and asked, 'Which do you want first, the good news or the bad news?'

I was told that they had finally detected my problem, but the solution, which involved implanting a defibrillator, was going to cost to me six lakh rupees!

I felt that we had been struck by a bolt of lightning. I had never possessed a fortune of this order. Indrani, on the other hand, just nodded to the doctor and said, 'Give me forty-eight hours and we can order the machine.'

She marched off to the nearest telephone booth to make some calls. The first to respond was my old friend VS Chauhan. He said, 'I don't have all the money but will get others to chip in.' Indrani's sister and brother also agreed to help. It is ironic that later my detractors were to accuse me of having amassed a fortune through corruption! And so, as promised, forty-eight hours later Indrani was signing the order for the defibrillator. The doctors, in the meanwhile, had another idea. They were going to implant me with both a defibrillator and a pacemaker, a first in medical history. I must confess that I felt a bit like a guinea pig.

On the day of the implant I was shaking like a leaf. Indrani, on the other hand, seemed supremely confident. The first night after the surgery was extremely painful, but the doctors felt that it had been a hugely successful exercise. A press conference was called and the surgery was widely reported.

Back in Lovedale, it was a matter of a few weeks before a multiplicity of problems began. I started to get shocks from the machine at the oddest times. The defibrillator was supposed to administer shocks only when the pulse rate went over a certain limit. Soon we were back to the hospital to have another surgery to sort out the problem. On my return, in a few months time the pacemaker site developed an infection which led to another surgery to remove the pacemaker.

When I returned after being declared fit, a wonderful event occurred in school. One afternoon I was informed by the piano teacher Mira Rodrigo that she had organized a small thanksgiving service in the school chapel. The choir would be singing a few hymns and the local pastor would conduct a service. Delighted, Indrani and I reached the church (Lawrence had a magnificent chapel complete with an organ and stained glass windows) at the appointed hour to find the school choir assembled and a smattering of faculty and support staff present. The choir sang beautifully while we occupied the first row and listened in rapt attention. The Pastor delivered a simple but dignified message of thanks. Although I am a cross between an atheist and agnostic, I was deeply moved. As we turned around after the service we saw that what had been hitherto a near empty church was now packed. The entire support staff and most of the local villagers had turned up. A large number of them came up and hugged me warmly. The one that stood out in my mind was Kuppuswamy, the head janitor, who with tears in his eyes hugged me and sobbed, 'Dorai, please never leave us!'

Little did I know that the storm clouds were brewing.

19

Trouble in Paradise

TOWARDS THE end of 1998, it seemed that the school had arrived at some sort of stability. By now we had more or less settled the disciplinary problems, our academic progress was reasonable and we had initiated several progressive educational measures. We could thus take off on our avowed mission to become the best school in the world.

There had been rumblings on the way. In 1995, a section of the alumni, had taken grave offence to my suggesting at a parent-teacher meeting that the Head should be allowed to implement his vision for the school without interference from anyone except the Board of governors. A senior alumnus visited me at my house and (fortunately) in the presence of two other parents warned me that if I did not leave the school, I would be crucified. The parents present were horrified at the impunity of the assault and took the matter up with the then Chairman Mr SV Giri.

Mr Giri was furious. He summoned me to his office in Delhi and told me that he was ashamed to be associated with a school whose alumni behaved in this manner. He said that I should not be cowed down by such threats and that I had his full support. The matter died down and I was able to establish cordial links with my detractors and indeed to convince them that we were both working for the same cause.

One of the wonderful things that happened to me as a fall-out of this incident was that I had the privilege of being befriended by one of the most remarkable men that I have ever known. Deepak Gera was one of the parents present when the emissary came to me with the message that I must leave the school. Deepak proceeded to take up the battle not only with the Chairman, but also enlisted the support of hundreds of other parents. As I did not know him at all at that stage I was rather intrigued and asked him why he did so.

'It's the principle of the thing,' he said. 'Nobody has the right to threaten anyone in this manner. If they have a genuine grievance there are appropriate fora where they can be addressed. This is not the way it should be done.'

Principles mattered to him more than anything else in the world. Over the subsequent years a very deep friendship developed between us and I learnt much as a result. It was a tragic loss when Deepak was suddenly snatched prematurely from our midst by a fatal heart attack. His wonderful wife Kiran still continues to be a friend and mentor.

In 1996 one of the governors (an alumnus as well) made a vicious attack on me at a Board Meeting, using unparliamentary language. The rest of the Board (with quite a few alumni on it) listened in shocked silence. He was later asked to resign.

However, as the said Board member had made some remarks about financial impropriety, I asked the Chairman to look into the matter seriously. A committee was appointed comprising T. Gundan, an alumnus and Board member, and a chartered accountant, to probe into the school's finances for any evidence of impropriety. I quote the conclusion of the report of this committee:

> *The committee is of the view that although there have been procedural lapses and lack of stage-wise approval there is no apparent misappropriation of any funds.'*
> *(17.03.2006)*

These rumblings apart, we seemed to be sailing along quite smoothly. However, there was one constant complaint that cropped up from the parents, particularly those from the defence services. Our board examination results were just not good enough for our students to compete against the best for admission to university.

While I have always been a believer in education turning out multi-dimensional individuals and not just academically successful ones, I could not turn a deaf ear to this grouse. As a matter of fact, I have always felt that it is students with a multiplicity of interests and skills who do well academically too.

Some serious introspection was, however, required to see how we could improve our board examination results. I held a series of meetings with my faculty and a variety of suggestions and ideas emerged. We decided to track the weaker students right from class nine onwards, provide extra academic tutorials, have special coaching camps for the board examination classes and so on. In fact, many of these measures were already being implemented.

The one elephant in the room, which, however, no one had been willing to acknowledge so far, was the issue of Founder's Day. It is very difficult to explain to anyone who has not been to Lawrence what the Founder's Day obsession is all about. It was scheduled in May each year, but the spirit was in the air as soon as students returned from home after the winter vacation in January. The final examinations (which were scheduled in March) were regarded as a minor irritant on the way.

Traditionally, it was the new class twelve who ran the preparation for the Founder's Day and it was the attempt of each batch to outdo its predecessor's performance. The celebrations themselves were spread out over three days in May, but the centrepiece of the entire event was the parade and the beating of the retreat. Every single student (unless medically exempt) had to participate in the parade and it was the duty of every guard commander (i.e. the boy in charge of each squadron) to ensure that his squadron was absolutely fine-tuned and faultless.

In a school of seven hundred students, there would obviously be some who lacked the motor skills required to march in unison with the rest. The guard commander could not have any of this. The students had to practise relentlessly in the burning sun, till they got it right. If they did not, much harsher measures were put into effect.

It was hugely prestigious to be part of the band. There were, as a matter of fact, three of them; a brass band, a pipe band (all girls) and a bugle band. Whilst the beating of the retreat was quite spectacular, the pressure to perform flawlessly was enormous and hours of practice went into the effort. It went without saying that in attempting to outdo the previous year's performance, the guard commanders and the band-leaders (amongst the boys), did very often exercise brute force. I remember having to deal with some seriously traumatised little drummer boys who had been beaten black and blue in order to get the best out of them.

The other issue was time. The demand to stop classes and concentrate exclusively on Founder's Day began the moment the final examinations ended in March. In my first year I was horrified to see that virtually from April to the middle of May (when school closed for the summer, just after Founder's Day), there were no classes. Over the years, I tried very hard to extend the working period in April, but the teachers complained that no one really cared about was what was happening in the classroom and students could hardly wait to get out for practise.

This was, by no means, an easy call for me. I was fully aware of the fact that parade and retreat were an integral part of the traditions of the school and something that the entire school community (including myself) was extremely proud of. Having been brought up in the army I appreciated more than most the importance of tradition. However, as an educator it was also my duty to provide the best possible opportunities to all students to compete with their counterparts from other schools in the cut-throat competition for admission to universities. We were losing more and more students each year from class ten. These students would seek admission to a day school which they felt would prepare them better for the final board examination of class twelve. I began wondering whether our students in this day and age could afford the inordinate time that they were spending on these activities? Somehow, a balance had to be found between tradition and the changing needs of the times.

There was yet another area where I had a philosophic disagreement (albeit a very personal one) with the entire business of military tradition. Somehow it seemed to me that with the education system itself already deadening creativity and stifling a spirit of inquiry, we, as a school, ought to be doing what we could to counter this trend, at least in areas over which the stranglehold of the curriculum did not exist. It appeared to me, however, that with all this emphasis on uniforms, hierarchy, marching and what-have-you, what we were doing was, in fact, creating a culture that was antithetical to encouraging creativity and a free spirit. Children, I felt, ought to be allowed to grow unfettered, to breathe freely, to be excited about expressing new ideas. After all, were these not the demands of the new world order?

In my discussions with some of the alumni the counter they posed was, 'But we all went through this system and are not any the worse for it.' What they were loathe to admit was that there were an equal if not larger number of them who had some very bad memories of what they had been through. And of course, I was always told that even Anjolie Ela Menon was a product of this very system. Of course she was, and of course she is, one of the greatest artists in the country, but how many Anjolie Ela Menon's might have slipped through the cracks because of the overbearing ethos of the system? And in any case, the boys school was far more 'militarized' than the girls.

In 1999 when we began to examine the problem of our board examination results, these issues began to be discussed for the first time. It was the unanimous opinion of the faculty that the time, energy and effort spent on parade and retreat were seriously impinging on classroom time. In August 1999, the autumn of our discontent, I decided to take the elephant head on. I wrote a letter to all the parents pointing out the problem created by the excessive emphasis on parade and retreat and sought their suggestions on this matter.

I concluded, 'Gandhiji once said tradition is like a river, we can choose either to sink or swim in it. The time has come for Lawrence to make the choice. I look forward to receiving your invaluable reaction to this letter.'

Hundreds of parents started writing in. Some were of the opinion that parade and retreat were seriously outmoded and should be scrapped. Others said that we ought to just scale things down a bit. Some were of the opinion that the present system be retained. Funnily enough, most of the opposition to the parade and retreat came from parents from the defence services!

What I had not anticipated was the virulent reaction from a section of the alumni. The net went viral with what was called 'Operation Fireball'. The single aim of this campaign was to see me removed from the Headmastership.

Some of the subscribers to this campaign said I was destroying the glorious traditions of the school, others said that I was a terror who ruled both staff and students through fear. It was alleged that I brutalized students. Funnily enough none of those who made the accusations had their children in school! Some pointed out that I had been wasting precious school funds on horse riding, not to mention my own time which should have been dedicated to the school. Some of the language used was enough to make anyone with any sense of decency cringe.

It did not end there. Indrani started receiving anonymous phone calls threatening me. The callers would say that they knew that I had a pacemaker and all that it needed was a magnet to neutralize it. My daughter was followed into the town, her photos taken and morphed. Matters got worse. Anonymous letters started arriving addressed to the student body, accusing me, amongst other things, of sleeping with the lady teachers and Indrani of sleeping with the men.

My mind, at that time, went back to a letter I had received from Admiral Raja Menon (husband of Anjolie Ela Menon) dated 15 September 1999, where he had written, 'It (the parade) teaches above all the manly qualities of "steadiness" which immediately differentiates a boy who has done drill from a lounging Delhi school product...'

If these were the 'manly' qualities that Lawrencians had imbibed from the parade, I wondered whether schools were better off with 'lounging' products who were at least morally upright?

Of course letters like this were bound to have a devastating effect on the family as both our girls would certainly have been told about them by their friends. I, for one, did not have the courage to address the issue. Indrani had to step in and she told the girls, 'There will be much more of this in the days to come. It is important that as a family we believe in each other and support each other.' Enveloped as we were by the storm, it was easy not to notice the hell that Diya and Shama must have been going through as students of the school. To their credit they remained stoic throughout. It was only much after we had left Lawrence that I discovered how embittered they were, bits of which persist even to this day.

The head of a nearby Christian school arrived one day and asked us to hold hands with each other in prayer. A parent insisted that we undertake a trip to the temple of Guruvayur to seek blessings. Whilst I am not particularly religious, I must admit that in those tumultuous times, I too found some succour in these acts of support. I had never imagined that a letter written in good faith, with no personal axe to grind and aimed at benefitting the current students entrusted by their parents to the school, would evoke such a reaction.

After all, had I not for the last eight years helped facilitate some of the finest Founder's Day celebrations the school had ever seen? I was also the first (and so far, at least, the last) Head of school to have actually allowed (in the face of much opposition, I may add), a girl student to actually command the parade one year, in tandem with the Headboy. I had also added to the glamour of the entire event by introducing the practice of the horse-drawn buggy and mounted escort for the Chief Guest.

As a matter of fact, one of the younger alumni at the height of the crisis wrote to the entire fraternity, 'Forget cancelling Founder's, we had some of the best Founder's under his [Mr Lahiri's] watch. I still remember my eighth grade Founder's, when in pouring rain the Beating Retreat was flawlessly performed while Mr Lahiri stood outside saluting and soaking wet the whole time, with the band.'

Moreover, I had never once suggested 'scrapping' Founder's Day. I just did not have the authority to do so. All I had suggested was that we have a re-look at the kind of time and effort that we were spending on this exercise in view of the intense pressure of having to improve the Board examination results. Whatever my personal beliefs on the absurdity of the 'marks syndrome', I felt that as head of school, I could not disregard the views of a large section of the parents.

In an attempt to stem the flood I called for an emergency meeting of all stakeholders so that we could hammer out some compromise and present our findings to the Board. Very senior alumni were invited, as was the executive committee of the Parent-Teachers Association (called the Friends of Lovedale Society) and the faculty. A lengthy discussion ensued and eminently sound advice was offered by the senior alumni present such as Jose Dominic and Viju Parmeshwar. It was agreed that all that should be done, at least to begin with, was to cut down on the parade and retreat and reduce the time given off for classes for Founder's Day.

The final paragraphs of the minutes read,

> 'The meeting expressed full faith in the Headmaster and the Staff and the commitment they had to the school and left it to them and the Board to effect whatever changes, however radical of the "Founder's Show", Parade and Band for the betterment of the school. The meeting concluded with an expression of appreciation for inviting an open dialogue and involvement of all stakeholders of the school.'

Armed with this input, I decided to meet the Board at the next meeting and seek their views. But Operation Fireball had, in the meantime, found two redoubtable leaders in Anjolie Ela Menon, the internationally renowned artist, and her sister, the late Nomita Chandy. I was completely nonplussed at this turn of events, particularly because both of them had been frequent visitors to my house and had been very helpful with suggestions and new ideas. Anjolie Ela Menon had indeed written to me as recently as the 19th Nov, 1999 stating, 'I am fully aware (and have been a vocal advocate) of the many great things you have done for the school.'

As a matter of fact, at that point of time I felt that Anjolie, her sister Nomita and her husband Admiral Raja Menon and I enjoyed a relationship based on mutual respect. The three of them would dine with me whenever they happened to visit Lovedale and we would discuss school and related matters quite freely and openly. Nomita and I were, in fact, in the process of finalizing a scholarship-based admission to Lawrence for an underprivileged child, sponsored by her Trust.

The much awaited Board meeting regarding Founder's Day was held and the Board ruled that the celebrations should carry on as usual. I dutifully recorded the instructions and relayed them to the school on my return. Imagine my surprise at receiving a letter forwarded by the Ministry of HRD, dated 26:11:99 signed by Anjolie Menon, her husband Rear Admiral Raja Menon, and her sister Nomita Chandy, in which they listed various allegations against me. These included 'misappropriation of funds, manhandling little children, including girls, being against the Bharatiya Janata Party (BJP) (the National Democratic Alliance led by the BJP was then in power) and making anti-BJP statements.'

While I had no idea where the first two allegations came from, I could see what might have led to the anti-BJP ones. Close on the heels of the brutal killings of the Staines children in Orissa, I had been instrumental in organizing a peace march of all Ooty schools to the office of the Collector. We had marched in silence and handed over to the Collector a petition signed by all the students participating that we wished to grow up in an India where such incidents would not occur and there would be peace and harmony amongst communities. I had also publicly denounced the destruction of the Babri Masjid, just as I had in 1984, while teaching at Doon School denounced the massacre of innocent Sikhs. But now, I was being beaten with that stick and by the so-called intellectual elite at that.

Meanwhile trouble was brewing on other fronts as well. While I was away at Bombay to meet RK Krishna Kumar, an ex-member of the Board, to seek his advice, T. Gundan, one of the Governors, visited the school with Nomita Chandy. I was informed that they had summoned a faculty meeting in my absence and let it be known that I was on my way out as Headmaster and that those amongst the faculty who wished to be in the good books of the new administration would have to sign a petition against me.

A petition, repeating much of what was being said in Operation Fireball, was drafted and sent to the Ministry and became part of the package of allegations against me. The fact that a large number of the signatories later recanted and wrote to the Board informing them of their disassociation with the petition was never taken into consideration.

The petition had been forwarded through Narayan Rao, a Governor. I warned Narayan, who was also a very dear friend, that should such petitions be entertained, it would spell the beginning of the end. Dev Lahiri, I said, would not be there forever, but whosoever occupied the chair of the headmaster would perhaps have that Damocles sword over his head once a precedent was set. My warning was to prove to be prophetic.

In the meanwhile about two hundred parents wrote letters of protest to the Ministry. The Head of the Association of Schools in the Nilgiris and indeed the entire support staff sent in their protest against Operation Fireball to the Ministry as well. Their feelings were best summed up in a letter written by Viju Parmeshwar, an alumnus and the President of the Parent-Teachers Association. On 17th December, 1999 he wrote (and I quote):

> '4. Mr Lahiri has been good for the school as it is a far better place than it was six or seven years ago. Further, he seems to be the only person amongst the staff that many parents can relate to. What will happen to the children now without him in the immediate short term, particularly for the tenth and twelfth standards who have to do a board examination in two months?'

It was ironic that there was no mention of my inflicting any brutality on the students as alleged by some of the old students, either in this letter, or in the two hundred odd letters written by the parents. The Board, however, had by now got caught in its own web of deceit and lies. AJ Tharakan, another alumnus and a member of the board, had written to me on 4th June 1999, (and I quote):

> 'Dear Dev,
> Please convey my congratulations to all your staff on the excellent results that Lovedale has obtained in the CBSE examinations. It is indeed very satisfying as a Board member to see the consistent progress that Lovedale is making towards academic excellence under your headmastership.
> I wish you continuous success.
>
> Yours sincerely
> Sd
> (Abe Tharakan)'

On 19 October 1999, AJ Tharakan once again wrote a mail, this time addressed to all the alumni, that read,

'As a consequence of this present financial condition of the school, children studying in Lovedale virtually live in medieval conditions. The dormitories are falling apart. The plumbing and electric wiring are archaic and require immediate replacement. Living conditions in the Senior, Junior, Prep and Girls Schools are just appalling and the dormitories virtually inhabitable(sic). The Board, Headmaster and the Staff are fighting a losing battle to upgrade these living facilities. The toilets in the Prep school and the Girls school have been upgraded to a certain extent. A central laundry facility and computer centres have been set up in the Senior school, Junior school and Girls school. Bullying, which had taken on frighteningly sadistic proportions has been stamped out. Credit for all this must be given to the present Headmaster.'

Now on 28 December 1999, the very same A.J. Tharakan wrote an impassioned plea to the Chairman asking for my removal. He claimed that I was 'a pathological liar', suffered from 'a persecution complex', flew into 'uncontrollable rages' and could not 'control myself'.

Operation Fireball had acquired a life of its own!

20

The Crisis Deepens

Two incidents took place in the months of December and January (in 1999 and 2000) while I was in Madras with the school equestrian team which was participating in the Junior National Championships.

The Ministry of Human Resource Development (MHRD) sent me a huge file of the allegations made by Nomita Chandy and her cohort of supporters. These allegations ranged from financial irregularities to violent and abusive behaviour. Official files had been stolen from my office (I later discovered the 'source' had fled to Dubai) and correspondence taken completely out of context, cut and pasted together in order to point of finger of suspicion at me. In some cases deliberate interpolations were also made to make it seem like I was misappropriating funds!

Aryamma Sunderam, one of the country's leading lawyers and an alumunus and parent of a current student at Lawrence School, jumped into the fray on my behalf. He was incensed at how blatantly some people had misused their positions of influence to conduct such an insidious campaign. He helped me carefully draft a reply to each one of the allegations, point by point and backed with extensive documentation. I sent the reply off to the Ministry, little realizing that no one would even bother to look at it.

Nomita Chandy had in her possession a photograph of me (and some others) posing over the carcass of a dead wild boar. The boar had been shot some years ago on the campus. It had half its face blown off by gunpowder put out by the villagers to protect their crops and in a moment of childishness I had agreed to pose for the photo. Now, Nomita alleged, I had poached the boar, completely ignoring the fact that with a pacemaker (and sometimes two) in my heart, I could hardly fire a powerful rifle.

Nonetheless, Nomita Chandy reported this matter to Mrs Maneka Gandhi and also had an article published in a newspaper. She wrote to the Chairman saying that considering this incident I had lost the right to remain in office of the Headmaster of Lawrence School.

In the meantime an emergency meeting of the Board was convened in early January. The Chairman suggested that since all the old Lawrencians on the Board felt that they could not work with me, I may as well resign. I informed him I was quite happy to do so, but would want my name cleared of all the bogus charges that had been levelled against me. General Kapoor, the Defence Services representative on the Board, chipped in on my behalf.

'Mr Chairman, you are offering a man who has allegedly made lots of money an opportunity to go quietly. If I had been in his place I would have grabbed the offer. But he is sticking his heels in and demanding an inquiry. Surely we owe that to him.'

It was decided that an inquiry committee headed by Mr Veeraghavan (Chairman of the Bharatiya Vidya Bhavan) and consisting of K.S. Sarma, an I.A.S. officer and Rashna Imhasly (an old Lawrencian who had already made her views in favour of my removal known) were asked to visit the school and conduct the inquiry.

On 11th January 2000, on the day of Pongal, I was at home having breakfast with a parent of the school and a dear friend, Capt Praveen Nanda (ex-Navy and affectionately known as 'Tiger'), when my staff informed me that the house had been surrounded by about thirty policemen. Forest officials entered the house with a search warrant. I was told that I was suspected of harbouring illegal trophies. The cops turned the house inside out but could not find a thing. All they did find were all the weapons belonging to the school rifle club (all duly licensed) and all the dummy rifles used for the parade. All these were, as a matter of practice, kept in my house for safekeeping during the vacation. The cops also found some ammunition, which, incidentally, I had inherited from my predecessors and since it was in excess of the amount allowed in the license, I was to be charged under the Arms Act!

The forest officials then unceremoniously loaded me into a jeep and took me off to a forest guest house for a couple of hours of interrogation. They kept asking me to confess to the shooting of the wild boar and I kept refusing. All through the interview the officer questioning me would receive calls asking him if he had made a breakthrough. He informed me that the calls were from a 'higher up' in Ooty who had links to the school. I could only think of Gundan, who happened to be the local MLA.

After a few hours of futile questioning and recording statements, I was brought back to my house. Tiger advised me that I should leave town immediately. It was a Friday he pointed out and since the courts would be closed the next day, the cops would definitely move to make an arrest. If I could be kept in jail over the weekend Nomita and her supporters (who by now included the old Lawrencians on the Board) could press for my dismissal.

Tiger and I went straight to Coimbatore and from there took a night bus to Madras. Early in the morning we arrived at Aryamma Sunderam's doorstep. He had already instructed his junior lawyer to receive us and to appeal for anticipatory bail. To our dismay, a lawyers' strike was declared on the same day. For the next few days, on Aryamma's advice, we moved from one sleazy lodge to another. We could have stayed in the Madras club, but as Aryamma pointed out, that would be the first place the cops would come to look for us.

Eventually four days later I had to appear for myself and was granted anticipatory bail. The one condition laid down was that I had to sign my presence at the B1 police station in Ooty every morning at eight. When I did turn up to fulfil that condition, the SHO sheepishly informed me that in most cases involving eminent citizens of the district, the practice was to take about fifteen to twenty signatures at a time to avoid harassing the individual. In my case, however, strict instructions had been issued (once again by someone high up in Ooty connected to the school), that I was to report every morning failing which I was liable to be arrested.

In February, the inquiry committee arrived. On the eve of their arrival I received a call from an ex-Stephanian and dear friend in the ministry, Abhimanyu Singh, who was a Joint Secretary.

What he had to tell me did not actually inspire me with any confidence about the likely outcome of this committee's visit.

What my friend had warned me about was further confirmed by the circumstances in which the committee arrived. I had received a letter from the Ministry on 11th February 2000 which said (and I quote):

'You are requested to make necessary arrangements for transportation of the above-mentioned members/officers from Coimbatore airport to Lovedale and back. Necessary board and lodging arrangements in Lovedale may also be made for which the expenditure will be borne by the school.'

It did not come as a surprise to me, therefore, when Gundan sent his luxury cars to pick up the committee and whisk them off to a posh hotel for their stay, in complete defiance of the ministry's directive. On the night of 16th February 2000, I received a call from K. S. Sarma from the hotel. He offered me a deal. I must resign and the enquiry would be called off. I was horrified.

'Mr Sarma,' I said. 'I thought that this was to be a fair enquiry on behalf of the Government of India. I am sorry but I'm not interested in a deal.'

With that the conversation ended.

The committee spent three days inspecting the records and interviewing people. I was more or less blocked out of the entire proceedings. A few days later another committee appointed by the army arrived on the campus. The school was on land that had originally belonged to the Ministry of Defence and there was still a quota and financial subsidy for children from the Defence services. It appeared that a large number of defence parents had requested an independent enquiry. This could have been avoided if the chairman had paid heed to my suggestion that a representative of the Defence Services be included on the Veeraghavan committee.

On 29th February 2000, a meeting of the Board was called in Delhi. As I waited in the Chairman's reception to be called in a peon arrived and handed me a copy of the Veeraghavan committee report. This was the first time I had laid eyes on the document. Before I even had time to open it, I was summoned inside.

'Mr Lahiri', asked Mr Kaw. 'Do you know what that report contains?'

'I am afraid not sir', I replied. 'I have not even had the time to open it.'

'Well let me inform you that what it contains is enough to reduce your family to begging on the streets for the rest of their lives. I suggest you resign straight away.'

'I am prepared to resign, Sir, but I think you should give me a little time to relocate. I have already applied for a job and the interview is tomorrow (I had applied for the headship of the Scindia School, Gwalior and the interview incidentally was on the next day). Besides, the board examinations are about to start and this resignation is bound to disturb the school.'

'Oh yes we know all about the job interview and we have made sure you do not get it. This will keep happening till you play ball. As for the board exams, do you think you are indispensable? You have a serious heart problem. If you were to drop dead this minute, do you think the examinations would stop?'

I sat there with my jaw dropping. Was I actually listening to a Secretary in the Government of India speak?

Just at this point, my cell phone indicated a message. A group of parents led by Pradeep Rajagopal, an eminent lawyer and a parent, were approaching the High Court in Madras for a stay on my call for resignation. In that moment I realized that the last thing I wanted was a legal standoff between the parents and the school. That would certainly not be my legacy. I resigned forthwith. The silver lining from this episode was the forging of a wonderful friendship with Pradeep and his wife which survives to this day.

21

The Battle Continues

As I walked out of the Chairman's office, I had decided that I may have lost the battle but the war to clear my name was to continue unabated. As I read the committee's report my resolve was strengthened. The report had clearly violated the principles of natural justice by not giving me time to read it before being summoned by the board. In addition it was vague, inconclusive and did not have enough substance in the charges levelled against me.

Veeraghavan acknowledged this a few years later, when in response to a query about the report from the Chairman of Welham Boys' School (where I was then employed as Principal), he wrote (letter dated 28th September, 2005), 'the committee did not find any clear evidence of misappropriation of funds by Shri Dev Lahiri.'

Determined to seek justice, I continued to knock on every door from the Prime Minister's Office downwards, going down the ladder since the day I left Lovedale in April 2000. Every Education Secretary would receive a request for representation from me and fortunately for me an interview was always granted. Despite the lack of concrete resolution to my problem, the matter was kept alive. Finally, in 2006, the Gowrishankaran Committee was appointed to have a close look into the issue and I was also asked to depose before it in Chennai. The subsequent report of the committee said:

'At the first instance, the committee met itself and deliberated on the Veeraghavan Committee report. It was felt that the said report is vague and there is no conclusive finding on any issue... The committee after hearing Mr Lahiri and perusing the papers on record came to the conclusion that though there are lapses and mistakes, maybe negligence, there seems to be nothing on record to show that Mr Dev Lahiri has indulged in misappropriation of funds. There have been cases of self-motivated decision-making on the part of Mr Lahiri, for example, in the case of horses and it appears to be a case of absence of procedure which ought to have been laid down by the Board. In the absence of procedure and keen interest that the Board of Governors ought to have taken in the affairs of the school, it is quite natural that the Head of the institution has to take decisions of his own which may appear to be lacking in propriety and procedure at a later stage. Therefore, the present committee is unable to swing the needle of suspicion towards Mr Dev Lahiri for lapses that occurred during his tenure of nine years in school.

'It is the considered view of the committee that the Board of Governors should be more alert in the performance of their duties and regulate and streamline the functions in a manner befitting the reputation of the school. It has been felt that in the past; except for participating in the meetings of the Board of Governors, the members seem to have hardly any interest in the development of the school and up-keeping (sic) its reputation... It is the recommendation of the present committee that certain introspection is required on the part of the Board of Governors for their laxness in the affairs of the school...'

And this was the Board that had forced my resignation!

The matter did not end here. I had been writing to the authorities of the Indian Army repeatedly requesting them to release a copy of the report of the inquiry that they had conducted in November, 1999. This had been steadfastly refused on the grounds that it was classified information. With the passage of the Right To Information (RTI) Act, I was able to approach the Central Information Commission, who ordered the army to release their report to me: Prepared by the Commander of the Madras Regiment Centre, Wellington (in parts), Stated and I quote:

'12. *Flash Pt of controversy for Present Headmaster:*
A letter asking the parents to change the format of Founders to devote more time for academic excellence achievement. No decision was taken, only debate was invited. The issue was simmering since 1991-1994 wherein the Headmaster had thrown out children of influential persons who were involved in ragging/bullying of juniors.

13. During Nov 99, old Lawrencians met the staff of the school and created panic in the staff by creating job insecurity, and projected that Dy Headmaster be promoted as new Headmaster (Mr Arun Dash). They alleged that Arun Dash was forced to resign by the present Headmaster, whereas the job of the Dy Headmaster was not confirmed by the Board of Governors due to inefficiency.

14. Parents are supporting Mr Dev Lahiri being

efficient Headmaster.

15. Mrs Nomita Chandy is leading the campaign against the present Headmaster. She is the sister of Mrs Anjali Ila Menon, w/o Rear Adm Raja Menon. Rear Admiral Raja Menon and his wife are old Lawrencians. However, Mrs Nomita Chandy has no connection with the school. She is running a school in Bangalore. It seems that the school is not doing well. It is renounced (sic) that Mr Arun Dash be appointed as Headmaster and subsequently be replaced by Mrs Nomita Chandy...

16. Wild boar was killed in the school in 1991 wherein the present Headmaster has been photographed with the killed wild boar. It is learnt that the wild boar was killed by one of the chowkidars. However, the present Headmaster got himself photographed with the wild boar, which has been leaked out to fix the responsibility of poaching on the Headmaster. An issue is being highlighted which is not connected remotely with the capability of the Headmaster. The issue of 1991 is being highlighted for vested interests.

17. Mr Dev Lahiri is considered an honest and efficient Headmaster and commands respect among students and parents. Service officer parents are quite happy with him. He has brought about qualitative changes/improvements in the school and made it one of the most famous schools of the country...

This was a victory indeed, but the war was far from over.

While all this was going on, the cases pertaining to the shooting of the wild boar and the Arms Act were still dragging on. Every now and then, I would be served a summons to appear in the lower court at Ooty. I was able to comply on some occasions (at considerable expense and inconvenience, as I was by then the Principal of the Welham Boys' School, Dehradun) and I was unable to attend the others. Aryamma Sunderam came to my rescue and with the help of a lawyer recommended by him I was able to get the case under the Arms Act quashed by the High Court in Chennai as late as 2009.

I was also corresponding with the then Chairman, M. R. Sivaraman, a retired IAS officer, in an attempt to recover the annuity payment that the school owed Indrani and me. In an e-mail dated 30th July, 2005, Sivaraman wrote to me (and I quote):

> 'I have not seen any accusation of cheating against you. Your being a Rhodes Scholar is indeed creditable and any school that has you should use you properly... What has failed in Lawrence is the supervisory system based on rules... The rules are scanty and full of loopholes...'

Sivaraman visited me at Welham Boys' and spent the better part of a day looking closely at some of the systems in place. He also addressed the school assembly, where he spoke about me in glowing terms.

Imagine my surprise, therefore, when in February 2008, when I found posted on the website of Lawrence School the minutes of a meeting of the Board held on 8th February 2008, wherein paragraph nine read:

> 'The board considered the reports submitted by the internal auditors on the various administrative and financial lapses alleged to have taken place in the school when Mr Dev Lahiri was the Headmaster.

> The Board concluded that there have been serious financial irregularities... Apparently, no action has been initiated against anybody for these lapses. As Mr Dev Lahiri, the then Headmaster, had left the school way back in the year 2000 there appeared to be no possibility of initiating any disciplinary action against him at this stage.'

A quick look at the composition of the Board and the motive became clear. A certain Moriarty was at it again!

I immediately wrote to Sivaraman informing him of my intention to sue for defamation in the absence of an apology. As no apology was forthcoming, defamatory proceedings were initiated. The trial court in Dehradun set a date for the hearing in October 2008.

On the day prior to the hearing, I received a call from Col Prasad, the then Headmaster of Lawrence School. It seemed that Sivaraman was with him for the hearing and wished to see me. I invited them to my office. Col Prasad came alone and as he was waiting in the reception area of my office, I received a call from a well-wisher informing me that there were ten policemen from Tamil Nadu at the local police station, with a non-bailable warrant for my arrest, for not having turned up for a hearing in the wild boar case. When I asked Col Prasad whether he had any knowledge of this, he went into denial and said that this was a mere coincidence!

However, he offered a way out. I should withdraw the defamation case and Sivaraman would ensure that the wild boar case was dropped. I politely asked him to leave my office, adding that I was quite prepared to fight the case as I had done no wrong. Sivaraman then called the media and had a field day telling them that I was an absconder from the law. The cops went back to Tamil Nadu after twiddling their thumbs in Dehradun for a few days.

Now it was my turn to make sure that the warrant was recalled. For that I had to appear before the magistrate in Ooty. It seems that the law, in such a case, says that I could still be arrested at any time before I actually entered the court premises. Some wonderful parents of my old students from Lawrence and some old students as well came to my rescue. Not only did they arrange for my stay in Ooty but also ensured that I got to the court without mishap. The warrant was finally recalled but not before Sivaraman had roped in the Press to publish stories about how a well-known wildlife offender had been summoned to the court in Ooty!

The wildlife case dragged on, as is usual in our system, till April 2012 when it was finally dismissed altogether. But it had taken its toll on my finances and peace of mind which I presume was the purpose of those who initiated it in the first place. I had to suffer, repeatedly so, the ignominy of appearing in a criminal court with common criminals. I wonder how proud the alumni felt about reducing an ex-Headmaster unjustly so, to this situation.

The defamation case, in the meanwhile, having passed through the trial court went up to the High Court in Nainital to be argued for its maintability. The lawyers appearing on behalf of Lawrence School made a spirited attempt to have it thrown out, but the Chief Justice of Uttarakhand (who heard the matter), ruled in my favour. The case would be heard.

Lawrence School now filed a Special Leave Petition in the Supreme Court. They had Gopal Subramaniam, one of the country's leading lawyers, representing them. For my part, an old student of mine from Doon School, Siddharth Dave, very kindly agreed to represent me and gratis at that. Siddharth carried the day and Lawence School's petition was turned down. The school would have to face defamatory proceedings.

At this stage I received a frantic telephone call from Col Prasad. By this time Sivaraman had resigned as Chairman of the Lawrence School Board. Col Prasad said that he had no stomach for a fight and had been involved against his wishes right from the start. Would I please agree to a compromise?

I told him that I had only fought as I had been forced into a corner and had to protect my reputation. I had no interest in a legal battle with a school that I had served for nine years. We met in the office of the Education Secretary in Delhi (where ironically it had all started). The school offered me my annuity and an apology (reproduced below):

The Lawrence School
(An Aegis of the Ministry of HRD, Govt. of India)
Lovedale, Ooty – 643 003
The Nilgiris, Tamil Nadu, (India)

Phone: 0423-2442282, 2442784, ██████████
Fax : 0423-2442640
Email: lawrenceschool@sancharnet.in
Website: www.thelawrenceschool.org

Date: 08 Feb 2010

Mr. Dev Lahiri,
Principal,
Welham Boys' School,
Circular Road,
Dehradun – 249 001
Uttarakhand.

Dear Sir,

I would like to reiterate the decision of the Board of Governors of the Lawrence School, Lovedale that it will not pursue any matter against you any more pertaining to your tenure as the Headmaster of The Lawrence School, Lovedale and also will not publish anything derogatory or accusatory in nature against anyone.

Yours faithfully,

Lt. Col. (Retd.) YHVS Prasad
Headmaster/ Member Secretary

The war was finally over. I felt no sense of triumph; only disgust and sadness that the high and mighty of the land were arrogant enough to believe that they could trample anyone underfoot at will. Perhaps the finest evocation of all that happened came from an old student of Lawrence, the late Dr Salim Firdaus, who had also been a parent of a child studying at the school during my tenure as Headmaster. In a message posted on the website on 12th September 2005 he wrote:

What does a man do when he is accused with a slew of crimes, some so heinous that the after shocks reverberate long after vindication- Embezzlement, Fraud, Child Molestation are serious enough for anyone to face. But, when these charges were framed on the Headmaster of Lawrence School Lovedale it behoved us with any sort of connection to Lovedale to have seen that this matter was disposed of, fairly and impartially, taking utmost care that only the core allegations were objectively dissected, before any sort of judgment was pronounced. We failed on this score- to insist on transparency and due process was impossible because the system failed us. We let the hysteria of Operation Fire Ball generated on the internet to build its own critical mass and allow the Bushes to hold sway.

From the Kafkaesque farce of the Inquiry committee, to the speed and grim certitude of Lawrence School Lovedales own Kangaroo court, what chance did Dev Lahiri have?

It has been five years for the man who was Headmaster of Lawrence School Lovedale to have been unceremoniously dumped into the cold after having been stripped of his last vestiges of dignity. Forced to live on hand outs from friends, every avenue of earning a livelihood barred by a vicious whispering campaign, with a young family and a serious heart condition, it took a long time for rehabilitation. But by then, the years in the wilderness had taken its toll. Nearly 12 surgeries (twice left for dead) its a miracle he is still around. He had used the time to knock on the doors on the highest bodies of education in the land and ask for a full review of his case.

Point for point, every accusatory statement was trashed out with overwhelming evidence to prove his innocence- without a shadow of doubt (THE ANNEXURES CARRIES THE SEQUENCE OF EVENTS AND ALL THE PERTINENT PAPERS).

The legal department by a special order from the PMO has found no instance of illegality.

The audits for those particular years certified that there were no financial irregularities, only procedural lapses. This was duly testified by an OL Governor of the Board.

The Chairman of the Board has not found one instance of any wrong doing when Dev was the head.

Another OL Governor of the Board had penned a laudatory testimonial on the good he was doing in Lawrence School Lovedale before her abrupt U Turn.

The scores of teachers who were coerced into giving false statements against their heads retracted them fully

Even as late as last year, Dev was invited to a Board meeting in Delhi to state his piece. He was heard out in stony silence. His demand this time was an apology from the people who caused him all this pain and misery and restitution of the amount owed to him by the school.

Here is a man living on borrowed time, neck deep in debt asking for no more than a acknowledgement of his innocence after being duly proved so from his erstwhile accusers and for the money unjustly held back so that he can gently pass into the night without burdening his family with debt and dishonour. When this was not forthcoming, the only recourse left to him was the courts of land in which cases were filed as far back as 2000 on the behest and guidance of an OL counsel of the Supreme Court.

If by pursuing the defamation case his chief documented accusers were put to the indignity of being hauled up in court, think of the man who headed the pomp, pageantry and esteem of LSL, being hounded like a common criminal, forced literally onto the streets with little hope of succour just for being out spoken, proactive and refusing to bow down to the vested interests of the powers - that - be, which invariably are drawn to institutions geared for fame and pelf.

For a man in Dev's condition, the last thing he will want is revenge. When all attempts at asking for redressal of the wrongs done against him had failed, this line of action seemed the only way to keep alive those dark days of 1999-2000 when a gross miscarriage of justice traumatised, so many in School.

We, all of us connected to LSL should be on guard to see that never again should we allow the school and its ethos to be sunk to such dark depths.

Even now, mature, rational and well meaning members of the LSL family should take steps in helping sort out and patch up the wounds of 2000.

In this instance, common friends of the accusers, Dev Lahiri and the school board could mediate and facilitate a meeting where all the ghosts of those tumultuous years can be finally laid to rest.

Salim

Dr. Salim Ibrahim Firdouse
HP: +91 94440 32997

I am often asked if I feel bitter about what happened with me at Lovedale.

The answer truthfully is no. But sadness and regret will forever colour my days there. Every day of my nine years there when I breathed in the air of the campus and revelled in its natural beauty, I became more and more convinced that this was one school that, given the right inputs, could lead the world in school education. As a matter of fact, Terry Guest, the international head of the Round Square Conference (an international fraternity of schools to which Lawrence belonged), described Lawrence School as 'a powerhouse of a school' after a visit to the campus.

What the school needed was a progressive mindset. I respect tradition, particularly because I have been brought up in an army family. Traditions give us character. I also believe that one cannot become a slave to tradition, especially those that come in the way of progress. Even today I am dismayed to see on social media that the main concerns of the alumni of Lovedale are issues such as why some statue is no longer where it was in their time or why the uniform has changed. No one seems to be concerned about the fact that there is a revolution going on in the world of education and that we owe it to our students to equip them with the skills they will need to compete in the global arena. Just placing a few computers in the classroom does not modernise education. Marching and retreat are great traditions and have their rightful place, but they cannot elbow out the time and space required for imparting skills meant for the 21st century.

My stints at both Lovedale and Welham have often made me reflect on the role of public schools (in the British sense of the word) in India's educational system. There can be no denying that in this hugely tuition driven culture, public schools appear like oases in a desert. A child has the opportunity to get out on to a playing field, or sketch on a canvas, act in a play or do something other than go through the grind of classroom and tuition, which seems to be the fate of most of our children today. In the process many skills such as those of being a leader and a team player, learning to accept defeat with grace and victory with humility are learnt. These are skills that are urgently needed in the professional world. Moreover, the friendships forged in boarding schools are friendships for life.

At the same time, it cannot be denied that the system faces serious challenges. There is, for a variety of reasons, a huge paucity of teachers in the country. Public schools, perhaps due to their geographical location and uncompetitive salary structures (compounded by the fact that day school teachers have access to a huge tuition market) are worse affected by this shortage. The rigid hierarchical structure (Prefectorial system etc.) that exists in these schools can often have serious repercussions. The 'senior-junior' pecking order very often results in bullying of various kinds and shades. This creates a climate of fear that stifles creativity and growth. In terms of their management some of these schools are in a world that has been left ages behind. They continue to live in a world dominated by the old boys mafia far removed from the professionalism that is the call of the day. Public schools have so much good to offer but they will have to seriously reinvent themselves.

As I write these lines, I look back on those tumultuous years and all that followed and my most fervent desire is that generations of Lawrencians read Dr Firdaus' letter and perhaps keep in mind the inscription I saw at the erstwhile German concentration camp at Dachau, 'NEVER AGAIN'.

22

In the Wilderness

As we drove out of Lovedale on 8th April 2000, for the last time, my mind went back to all the bitter events of the last few months. Yet the memories which remain etched in my mind are those of the last two days of our stay there.

On the evening of 7th April, the entire school, in defiance of the administration's orders, trooped into our residence to bid farewell. The Head Boy and Head Girl had arranged to present a lovely watch to us and many tearful speeches were made. What really floored me was when almost the entire school lined up to touch our feet. For a school steeped in military tradition this was indeed a quantum leap in an entirely different direction!

Our relationships forged with some of our old students have survived to this day. As a matter of fact, a few years ago, I was in urgent need of funds for my defibrillator replacement and it was one of my ex-Head Boys who arranged to raise close to six lakh rupees for the procedure! More recently, an ex-Head Girl wrote to us saying that she wanted us to meet our 'granddaughter' (her daughter) and that she was sending us two tickets to make the trip. Yet another memorable moment was provided a few years ago when one of our old students from Lovedale phoned to say that his batch had decided to raise some funds for their alma mater. In deciding what they would raise funds for, they felt that it would be best if they were guided by a sense of what their Headmaster (i.e., me) would have wanted to have the money for. The result? They raised money to provide the school's support staff (who are largely forgotten during any fund-raising endeavour) with toilets! I could not have asked for a greater tribute. These are relationships that Operation Fireball could not take away from us.

One of the most heartwarming sights I saw a few days before I left and perhaps proof of our 'success' (though that is better left for history to decide) at Lovedale, was that of the then Head Boy walking up the slope to senior school with a junior perched on his shoulders. Never had I imagined when I joined the school in June 1991 that I would ever see such a sight at Lawrence. It made all the trials and tribulations seem worthwhile.

Then on the morning of the 8th April, as we were getting ready to leave, the entire support staff turned up at our doorstep and demanded that we attend a church service with them. On our way to the church, I saw a flag fluttering above the support-staff club house. When I asked what that was about, I was told, 'Dorai, now that you are no longer there to look after us, we have had to form a union.'

Later as we got into our car to leave I looked back to check if the van with all our belongings and our dogs was ready to leave. Oddly enough, I found it crowded with people as well. Apparently, almost the entire maintenance department had decided to accompany us to Bangalore, where we were headed, because they had been told that the house we had rented there was in bad shape! Yet another defeat for Operation Fireball!

But it was not only the house in Bangalore that was in bad shape. My entire life and that of my family lay in shambles. I had no job, virtually no savings and I had to pull out my daughters from school at a critical time of their lives (my younger daughter was in class eight and the older one in class twelve). The two, though they had put up a brave front through it all, had been seriously traumatised. Almost overnight they had been wrenched out of the life and surroundings they had virtually grown up in and packed into a car heading for a strange city and an uncertain future.

As if to rub salt into our wounds, our truck was stopped at the Masinagudi check post. The Ranger, a kindly man, informed us that they had received instructions (from some higher up in authority in Ooty, connected to the school) to unload our truck on suspicion of smuggling ivory and to ensure that we received no help to reload it. I still wonder what prompted such vengeful feelings. Of course, I had made mistakes during my stewardship of Lawrence School. Yet were they of such a heinous nature to attract such retribution?

I like to believe that sometimes divine justice has its own poetic devices. About a year later, I read a newspaper report that a certain higher up authority in Ooty, who also happened to be an MLA, was stripped, beaten and plastered with cow dung by the very people of his own constituency.

There had, however, been no divine intervention in my matters till then, barring one. My old and dear friends from my college days, Pratap and Anita Reddy, came to our rescue. Pratap was a businessman in Bangalore and Anita ran an NGO called Awaas, which provided housing to the urban poor. Anita had arranged for me to work for her NGO as I tried to rebuild my life. What she was doing was ensuring was that I received a salary to sustain us, without losing my self respect. In the meanwhile I could cast my net around for something more appropriate given my professional experiences.

While I was looking around for a job, yet another heartwarming event took place. About half a dozen of the finest faculty from Lawrence put in their papers and four of them arrived in Bangalore to cast their lot with me. Only when one has been a teacher can one appreciate what courage it takes for an individual to give up a well-paid job in a residential school (with all its perks such as free accommodation, meals and education for children), pull their children out and head into a situation where there are no guarantees all for the sake of a principle.

Dr Gopalakrishnan, who ran a chain of schools in Bangalore, was only too happy to have them on his rolls at salaries much higher than they could ever think of in Lovedale. Since jobs for Headmasters are few and far between (this was before the school boom hit the country), I had to satisfy myself with working for a firm that produced educational software. If there ever was a low point in my life, it was this. To sit and type content for a website was not why I had become an educationist. Cut off from young people, confined to an office, I was starved of oxygen. There were even times when I thought of ending it all. It was only the resilience of my family and the support of friends such as Pratap and Anita and Tiger Nanda that kept me going.

One day I received a telephone call from Gulab Ramchandani, the ex-Headmaster of Doon School, under whom I had started off my teaching career and who was now an educational consultant. It seemed that an ex-IAS officer was keen to start a residential school outside Dehradun and was looking for someone to run it.

Would I be interested? It was like asking a caged animal if it wanted to be set free!

It was indeed a sense of great freedom to be on the train to Dehradun. Two old Stephanian friends, Ravi Singh and Zubair Ahmed, chipped in to provide the funds to make the journey as what the new employer was offering would not be enough to get the whole family across.

Setting up the Selaqui School (the school took its name from the village in which it was located), was initially a very exciting task. The salary was understandably not very princely (the school had not yet been built) and most of the work involved running around after various government agencies securing permissions, chasing contractors to deliver on time and look into all the nitty-gritties a project of this nature demanded. Closer to the scheduled opening, I was asked to recruit faculty. Who would I turn to other than my faithful band who were just biding their time in Bangalore for such an opportunity? Within days of my asking, P. Suresh, Srivalsan (SVM, as he was more popularly known), Nilendu Deb, Saikat Sarkar and Maria, a nurse, relocated to Dehradun with their families. A more professional, loyal, committed and visionary group I could not have asked for.

As funds were short, we all lived in the same house. This was quite an experience what with ten adults, four grown up children and three dogs sharing the same accommodation. The physical discomfort was more than made up for by the camaraderie and the excitement generated by the prospect of creating a new school. Late night discussions on the philosophy of the school and on the systems that would be required to put this philosophy into practice became the order of the day. And no one hesitated to perform any task required, from scouring the countryside for the appropriate plants for the gardens, to shopping for utensils for the school kitchen, to planning curriculum; no task was too small or too demanding.

Slowly, however, as the first students trickled in, it became evident that the management had a philosophy that was not quite in consonance with ours and certainly not what we had been led to believe would be the philosophy of the school. It was at this time that my health problems raised their ugly head. The site at which my defibrillator was implanted developed an ugly infection leading to a huge abscess developing in the area, accompanied by fever and chills. If not treated, it could prove fatal. So off I went to Bangalore where I would have to undergo a seven hour surgery. The situation was made a little more difficult by the fact that I got no chance to recuperate and had to rush back to Dehradun for the opening of the school. Indrani was literally hanging on to the last bottle of the antibiotic drip as we drove to the airport!

It was clear, however, that my health was breaking down under the stress. There were times when overcome by weakness, I would nod off at the steering wheel of the car. The doctors opined that I should be living in close proximity to good medical facilities. This along with the fact that we were all becoming rapidly disillusioned with the direction the school was taking, prompted me to turn to Shomie Das, my mentor, for help. He, in turn, was able to place me as Principal of the new Heritage school in Kolkata.

So began yet another epic journey, this time with two horses as part of the entourage. My old friend and supporter, Khusroo Dhunjibhoy, had very kindly sponsored two horses for me as he said that he found it very difficult to believe that I had to live a life with a heart affliction and no horses to boot! My colleagues too peeled off in different directions, some even choosing destinations overseas. With their impeccable credentials, they were able to secure good placements of their choice. I myself had learnt a lot from them and would miss them sorely. But the time had come to chart different paths.

23

Oh Kolkata!

Kolkata was a culture shock in more ways than one. In those early days we were accommodated on the fifth floor of a multi-storey building. The only view available was straight into the flats across and below us, where every evening we were treated to the sight of a rather portly Sikh gentleman stripping to his underwear to beat the heat. Soon we were able to move to more congenial surroundings in Salt Lake.

The Heritage School was a day school. The junior section, fully operational by then, was headed by a dynamic lady called Meenakshi Atal. In her I found a great friend, confidante and advisor. The friendship survives till this day. I was completely new to the day-school culture and needed much as much hand-holding in the scheme of things as I could get. Looking back, I doubt if I would have survived even the one year that I did had it not been for Mrs Atal.

The faculty for the most part was made up of ladies who were cheerful, hardworking and created a congenial work environment. I distinctly remember how ill-at-ease I felt when I walked into the first faculty meeting only to face forty women all ready for the meeting to begin.

The problem lay the management of the institution. The school had been set up with substantial financial contributions by a group of wealthy businessmen of the city. Therefore they felt entitled to call the shots. The problem was that the shots were often at cross purposes, especially when it came to admissions. I remember distinctly one occasion when a candidate had applied for admission, recommended by a famous film director and backed by one of the Trustees. Another Trustee, however, called me and told me that under no circumstances was I to accept that candidate. It took all of Meenakshi Atal's tact and diplomacy to resolve the impasse. Instances like this occurred quite often in various areas of the school's life.

The style of management irked me. Being from a public school background, I was not used to a Trustee shouting at me. To be told rather rudely that I must wait outside with the peon to be summoned into the office of the Secretary was something I found difficult to swallow. But I had to put my pride aside as I needed the job desperately.

The faculty, however, were a great team to work with. Many of them were hugely innovative and all of them, despite the long hours, kept a smile on their faces. Indrani too joined the school and very soon we were part of the family. I learned a great deal about the nuances of working in a day school from my colleagues, not least of all, Meenakshi Atal. It was a different dynamic altogether.

Through this learning curve, I however missed being in a residential school immensely. There were times when the 'withdrawal symptoms' became so acute that I would drive back to school after dark and patrol the premises with my dogs.

My health was failing. I felt terribly weak and was prone to sudden bouts of shivering even at the height of summer. I was also losing weight at an alarming rate. A friend advised me to seek a second opinion as the health services I were using in the city were not delivering tangible results. Dr Devi Shetty had himself examined me on some of his visits from Bangalore, but the problem persisted. So Indrani and I went off to see Dr Debal Sen, one of Kolkata's renowned cardiologists.

Dr Sen examined me, heard my history and said, 'Mr Lahiri, what you have is a life-threatening condition called endocarditis. Put simply, your heart is infected. And unless you get admitted to an ICU straight away for six weeks of intravenous antibiotic therapy, you are putting yourself at grave risk.'

Indrani and I were knew that six weeks of leave from the school would not be a possibility. We went back home quite devastated and started debating our options. There did not seem to be too many. As it turned out, the decision was taken for us. Two days later, as I sat watching the night time news on the television, I felt as if someone was stabbing me in the back. I screamed and Indrani ran in from the kitchen. The pain was excruciating.

We knew that Dr Raghuvanshi from the R. N. Tagore Hospital lived a few floors above us. Indrani grabbed the phone and told him what was happening. He was down in a flash and within minutes had bundled me into his car and sped to the hospital. I was rushed into the ICU and administered huge quantities of sedatives. It was indeed endocarditis that I was suffering from.

In the morning, as soon as I regained consciousness, I phoned the Secretary of the Trust that ran the Heritage school and informed him of my predicament. I apologized profusely for my inability to apply for leave in advance and assured him that I would try and get back to work the next day.

The Secretary cut me short and said, 'Mr Lahiri, I am afraid that we have no place for a sick man. Please treat this day as the beginning of your three months notice period.'

Indrani and I sat in the ICU with our heads in our hands. Our whole world was collapsing around us. Where would we go in three months' time? Our daughters were still in school and college. They had suffered enough with all our relocations. Indrani, for one, was not going to be beaten quite so easily. She immediately got on the phone to all those we felt could help. Mentors such as Shomie Das and Gulab Ramchandani were called and they all promised to do what they could.

We had, however, to deal with the immediate situation as well. There was the notice period to be served out and the Secretary was not going to yield any ground on that. I had myself released from the hospital, much against the wishes of my doctors and decided to undergo the intravenous antibiotic therapy while attending school. What this meant was the doctors stuck a large needle in my vein, protected it as best as they could and had me visit the hospital each evening for an hour of the drip. I was warned that the chances of picking up an infection through the needle were very high.

The large doses of antibiotics I was taking totally ravaged my system. By midday, I was slowed down and by evening I was in 'reverse motion.' It was as much as I could do to go home from the hospital, shove a few morsels down my throat and fall asleep. The stress this put on Indrani was quite unbelievable. She had to walk the three dogs (one at a time), do all the household tasks on her own, attend to school work and nurse me at the same time. Guilty as I felt there was nothing I could do.

It was during this period that the Welham Boys' and Assam Valley Schools advertised for positions of a Principal. I shot off my applications and we both kept our fingers crossed.

On 15th May 2003, I relinquished my office at Heritage School and was officially unemployed. The management very kindly allowed me to retain the flat till 15th August and that was the time frame I had to find myself a suitable job.

Assam Valley School was the first to call me for an interview. Before that, 'Pintu' Khaitan, the 'big boss' of Assam Valley himself, had invited us to the Bengal Club for tea where we discussed the school extensively. The buzz was that I had got the nod. The subsequent interview was in Delhi.

At Delhi as I finished what I thought was an eminently satisfactory interview and headed for the Roychowdhury's were I was staying, I received a call from Indrani in Kolkata saying that the recruitment firm that was looking for a Head for Welham Boys' had called and upon knowing that I was in Delhi at the time had expressed a keen desire to meet with me. I thereupon dropped by their office at Sunder Nagar where we had a long exchange of views and I was told that I would have to present myself in Dehradun for an interview. Meanwhile 15th August was fast approaching and our lien on the flat was running out.

On my return to Kolkata, I discovered to my bemusement that Assam Valley had decided not to make me an offer. That did not even bother me as much as the fact that that they did not bother to inform me and had I not taken the trouble to call I might never have found out. At this point Welham

Boys' School was the only card left in my pack as the August deadline approached. After some anxious moments post the interview in Dehradun, I landed the job.

Happy times however did not seem to last. As I finished the celebratory dinner at my father-in-law's home on my return to Kolkata after the successful interview, I felt a shock in my chest as the defibrillator went off. Pretty shaken I sat down to recover when the machine went off again. Indrani quickly got me into the car and with our daughter Diya drove to the hospital. On the way the machine went off seventeen times and each time it felt like a mule's kick in the chest. I was thrown from one end of the car to the other, screaming in fright and agony.

I found myself in the ICU once again. The next morning after reassuring me that the defibrillator was merely doing its job they let me go, certifying me fit to take on my new assignment. On 10th August 2003 we drove into the Principal's cottage in Welham Boys' School to begin yet another chapter.

24

The Welham Chronicles

IN THE course of my first few months at Welham Boys', I was beset by a sense of deja vu. Like Lawrence Lovedale, the school seemed to be in a fairly precarious condition. The academic results were woeful (as many as five boys had failed the previous year's Board examinations), the disciplinary fabric appeared to be in tatters with serious complaints from several quarters about the presence of cigarettes, alcohol and drugs on the campus. To make matters worse, the faculty presented a picture of near complete apathy with most of them busy raking it in with private tuitions, and the administration obviously needed a complete overhaul.

I can never forget the faces of the irate parents who met me at the first PTA demanding that I spell out a time frame for the improvement of the school. As one of them put it, 'Our children feel that school is where they come for a holiday and home is where they have to work!'

As I sat down to prioritize my action plan, I realized that the greatest threat to the school was posed by the menace of drugs. It was not just a question of the school. It was a question of the precious lives of young people. There had already been at least one casualty, with a young boy (a star soccer player at that) who had lost his life in a gang war in his first year at university.

The starting point for this crusade came when some of the faculty and I were able to identify ten students as being hard-core users. I reported the matter to the Board and it was decided at the next meeting that these ten offenders would be asked to leave the school. I was really torn by this decision. On the one hand I knew that the Board was only trying to strengthen my hands by sending out a very clear signal and on the other, I felt awful that almost the first thing I was doing after taking over was sending ten young men off without even trying to work with them.

In desperation I called the Chairman, Darshan Singh (himself an alumnus), and asked for permission to rescind the decision. To his credit, Darshan Singh backed me despite serious reservations expressed by many of the Board. This was the beginning of a long and mutually supportive relationship which unfortunately exploded most inexplicably several years later. But that was in the distant future.

The immediate problem was to deal with the ten boys. After much brainstorming with Indrani I decided that we had to treat this as a great opportunity. If these ten boys could be weaned off the habit we could use them to spearhead our campaign against drugs. Several sessions of discussions began with these boys. At the same time, guardians from amongst the faculty and indeed their own peers were appointed to monitor them on an almost minute to minute basis. The services of a local NGO Nijaat, which dealt with this problem were enlisted. The boys were counseled by, amongst others, ex-addicts who had kicked the habit. They were put under constant pressure to perform, both in the classroom and outside it. In an attempt to keep them engaged I gave them an old video camera and asked them to produce a news program on the school every fortnight. This was the humble beginning of 'Welham Newz' which has since then gone on to become an iconic institution in the school to which every Welhamite aspires to belong. Slowly but surely the ten boys started turning around.

Gradually the campaign, led by these ten, spread out to the entire school. Puppet shows, films, talks and workshops were organized on a regular basis. A few amongst these boys got together with their friends and produced a feature film to spread awareness. The film proved to be a very powerful instrument.

Strong-arm tactics were used to crush the source of supply. I was very fortunate in finding the support of A. B. Lal, a very senior police officer, who took this up as his own cause. Mr Lal himself conducted several workshops as part of this campaign. Police men in plain clothes were deployed around the school as decoys to trap the suppliers. I will never forget waiting with the cops one freezing night while two decoys went into the support–staff quarters of a neighbouring school from where we suspected that drugs were being supplied. Indrani and I started walking around the campus late at night with our large German Shepherds to deter would-be suppliers who would throw the stuff across the wall and flee.

This battle, I quickly realized, could not be won without the support of the parents. I, therefore, shot off a letter to all parents apprising them of the problem we had and asking them to exercise one of the two options available to them, withdraw their son from the school or help the school fight the menace. Some parents did exercise the first option but most were willing to help. We asked them to keep a close eye on their sons during the vacation and report untoward signs, if any.

The biggest weapon we had, of course, was the students themselves. The original ten had by then completely kicked the habit. It helped that amongst them were some of the school's outstanding achievers, both in academics and sport. When they spoke, others listened. The film that some of them had helped make became a powerful propaganda tool in their hands. Eventually we came to a stage when we were able to get the entire school to take a pledge that Welham Boys' would never allow even the shadow of this problem to fall across the school again and each one of the boys would look out for the other. I am proud to say that the rest of my tenure was never troubled on this particular score.

Part of the problem with Welham Boys' was that the school was struggling under the shadow of its more famous neighbour, the Doon School. Welham would have to develop a sense of pride and identity of its own. For a school close to seven decades old, it had surprisingly few traditions of its own. Here was an irony indeed! Whereas in Lawrence School, I was fighting the deadweight of tradition, at Welham I was struggling to establish some new ones. Over the years we instituted the Prefects' investiture ceremony, and the graduation ceremony and the high table, amongst others, became integral parts of our new traditions. It was also a singular triumph to induct the first girl Prefect at Welham Boys'.

Drugs was not the only disciplinary problem. The senior boys were a law unto themselves and went into the town without permission at will, including late at night. That was the least of their sins. The security systems had to be strengthened, the guards made less prone to taking bribes and the compound walls less scaleable.

However, it was the mindset that had to change for anything lasting to happen. I was shocked when, during my first few weeks in school, I saw the Prefects line up the entire school outside the dining hall and ask them to assume the 'murga' position in full view of the entire faculty. Clearly drastic measures were necessary.

Thus began the entire crusade to move away from the culture of physical punishment to measures more humane and progressive. The creation of a disciplinary committee with student participation, the introduction of a whole new code of conduct, of a system based more on reward than punishment, were some of the measures introduced. Chronic smokers were, for instance, as part of their rehabilitation, asked to go and live in the junior dormitories and look after the little boys. It was very rewarding to see the kinder side of their natures being drawn out in these circumstances.

The disciplinary problem sometimes took on strange proportions. In January 2004, while I was recovering from an open heart surgery, a distraught housemaster called reporting that a group of boys from class twelve who were appearing for the Board Examinations, had entered into a deal with some local boys to gain access to leaked examination papers. When they went to the exam hall they were bitterly disappointed to see that they had been duped. That night they scaled the school walls armed with hockey sticks to extract revenge from the perpetrators of this fraud. Not having found the boys concerned they had satisfied themselves by vandalising a car and some property. In retaliation a huge mob armed with sticks and chains had gathered at the school gates.

While advice to call the police was being flung my way, I realized that summoning the police could backfire very quickly if the situation took an ugly turn. Besides, our boys had started the trouble in the first place. I went up to the gate and asked to see the leaders. I assured them that I was alone and as Principal would address all the issues raised by them. I presume the sight of me completely strapped up after my open heart surgery had some impact. Three of the leaders stepped into the campus. I told them to go into the dorms where I had all the boys from class twelve assembled. Once they identified the culprits I assured them that the disciplinary committee would meet immediately and these boys were to face possible expulsion. At this point two of the leaders turned around to me and pleaded that I should not be so strict. They too had younger brothers sitting for the board examinations and knew how critical this juncture was in their careers. All they wanted was an apology and compensation for the damage to the car and property. This I promised to do the next day and the mob wound its way back to the town!

Problems of discipline also arose from the fact that the students were not being challenged enough, either academically, or on the sports field, or even in their co-curricular program. A multi-pronged campaign had to be launched.

Most of the teachers lived off the campus and as soon as classes gave over at lunch they headed back home (mainly to take private tuitions), leaving the responsibility for the students on the few who lived on the campus. The first step, therefore, was to ban private tuitions during term time. Henceforth, even during vacation, a teacher of the school could not tutor a student of Welham Boys' School. I had come across at least one case where a teacher had hired a hall in town and would leave his classes in school to a substitute while he took batches of students for private tuition during the hours he was to spend in the school.

The time table was restructured so as to require the presence of all faculty on the campus till at least six in the evening. Regular academic tutorials were organized; students were encouraged to collaborate on academic projects and once a month such projects were demonstrated to the entire school. Some of the finest projects that I have seen anywhere in the world resulted from this programme. Regular professional development for teachers became the order of the day. 'A faculty retreat' at the beginning of each academic term, at a location away from school, became the accepted practice and the brainstorming at these retreats resulted in serious improvements in our systems, both academic and administrative. 'Theme-teaching' was introduced whereby a common theme was taught across all classes irrespective of the subject for a specified period. Some of the most impressive exhibitions that I have seen were put up on Founder's Day as a result. There seemed to be a distinct joy in the learning process, both for the teacher and the taught.

Art, craft and indeed sports were allotted the same pride of place as academics in the school's priorities. 'Welham Newz' became so professional that that even experts from NDTV marveled at the technical skills the boys displayed. The Model UN was introduced in Welham Boys' long before any other school in Dehradun even thought of it. 'Bloom's Taxonomy' and 'Gardner's Multiple Intelligence' became buzzwords amongst the faculty.

The results soon started to show. Our board examination results went into an upward swing. We started excelling at sports. The prestigious Afzal Khan Basketball trophy (a tournament from which we were actually banned for a while on account of bad behaviour) now started finding a regular place on our shelves. In an effort to promote our national sport Welham Boys' started hosting the Kandhari Memorial Hockey Tournament (in memory of 'Charlie' Kandhari, one of the most illustrious ex-Principals of the school).

The trickle-down effect of all this on school discipline was amazing. The students were being so stretched in every direction that no one had the either the time or the inclination to host the 'devil's workshop'. This success made them hungry for more success.

All this was being accomplished in close cooperation with the Board, more particularly the Chairman, Darshan Singh. In sharp contrast to Lawrence School here I could, and did, approach the Chairman on almost a daily basis and he would craftily pilot all my suggestions through the Board.

In the midst of all this frantic progress I kept asking the school and myself one question, 'Why should the average man on the street be proud of Welham Boys'? What value do we add to the lives of the people who live around us?'

It was in response to this question that the school took on several initiatives. Amongst the earliest of these was our partnership with the village of Jaidwar in the Chakrata hills. The school undertook several projects there in collaboration with the villagers such as a community centre for the women, a playing field, improved water supply and eye camps, amongst other such initiatives. A deep, abiding friendship developed with the villagers as a result and some of our faculty and students were even invited to the village headman's son's wedding! We dedicated one entire Founder's Day program to fund-raising for the village and the children from Jaidwar put up some wonderful performances depicting their life and culture for our guests.

It was our program of street theatre, however, that really set us apart. Determined to take the crusade against substance abuse out into the town, the boys helped by an NGO,' Nijaat' launched a series of 'nukkad nataks' (street plays) across the length and breadth of Dehradun, targeting evils such as drug abuse and alcoholism. These were heartwarming performances, with the boys preparing their own scripts and then publicising their efforts with a simple portable loudspeaker and a drum. I sometimes wondered whether I, at their age, would have had the courage to sing and dance in front of a crowd in the middle of town. We also established a partnership with a Municipal school and the boys visited the school regularly to teach and play with the children there. Then one day someone had a great idea. Why not do a play on Founder's Day together?

An adaptation of 'The Lion King' was to be performed. Auditions were held. The part of the lion went to one of the boys from the Municipal school whose father made his living by selling vegetables. The rehearsals were scheduled every afternoon and all was going well until the eve of the final rehearsal which was to be held in the late evening as indeed was the final performance. On the eve of the final rehearsal I was visited by a rather irate father of the lion.

'Sir,' he said, 'you are taking my son away for two evenings when he is supposed to be pushing our vegetable cart all over the town. How will we compensate for this loss?'

The next morning I called the cast of the play together and apprised them of the problem. They would have to find a solution themselves if they wanted to put up the play. By the afternoon the problem had been cracked. The solution was to pool in all their precious pocket money and buy out the entire vegetable cart for the two evenings! The vegetables were to be dutifully handed over to the school kitchen. I doubt if any classroom or even MBA program could have taught them all that they learned from just this one experience.

The greatest sense of joy and fulfilment Indrani and I felt at Welham resulted from our interaction with one particular student. This was a boy in class eleven who was not only an outstanding student but an equally accomplished sportsperson and quizzer. More importantly, he was a very deep thinker and given to serious introspection.

One summer he returned from his vacation and appeared to be highly distracted and disturbed. His teachers reported that he had even stopped eating his meals in the dining hall. Seriously concerned, I called him home. As it happened Indrani was his history teacher and the two shared a good relationship. After much cajoling he told us that his mother had sent him during the vacation for some religious instruction. The priest entrusted with this task had told him that he was surrounded by impure people and that his mission was to cleanse the world of these impurities. He had utmost faith in the priest who he now saw as his mentor.

Indrani and I spent days with the young man trying to

convince him otherwise. We got ourselves a copy of his holy book and read it with him to show that nowhere was there mention of the things he talked about and that it was largely a question of human interpretation. We even invited parents of boys who shared his faith to counsel him. I then sent him to Delhi where a friend of mine from my university days was able to get him to speak to several eminent jurists of that faith. All to no avail. The boy's father visited school on more than one occasion but finally had to admit defeat and withdraw his son. Indrani and I were devastated. We considered this episode the single greatest failure in our professional lives and worried incessantly about where this young man might end up.

Years passed. I suddenly got a call from the young man. He was now a journalist, though his parents had forced him to study engineering. He told me that he had always wanted to study the humanities because he enjoyed Indrani's classes so hugely. He then went on to say that over the years he had learnt that every word Indrani and I had spoken to him was true. That there was no place in this world for bigotry and narrow-mindedness and that genuine happiness for all lay in peace and tolerance. He was now saving his pennies in order to be able to visit us. This indeed was our finest moment!

25

The Struggles

WHILE MUCH progress was being made in dragging Welham Boys' out of the shadow of the Doon School and giving it an identity to be proud of, there were still other battles to be waged. At the time I assumed office in 2003 I had been warned that Welham had perhaps the most powerful union of support staff in the state. As a matter of fact, three top functionaries of this union were indeed leaders at the state level. Although there were no apparent issues of discord I knew from the start that it was a question of time before I would be tested.

The union, or rather its leaders, however, had made a rather poor choice of issue to test me. This was the issue of the dhobis (washermen, who do the laundry). Welham Boys' had, from its very early days, been serviced by a group of local dhobis who washed all the students' clothes. They were not employees of the school nor were they on any formal contract. The relationship was based on an unwritten understanding much as one has with one's neighbourhood dhobi. The school provided the site and the water for this exercise. The dhobis were paid for each item of clothing that they washed.

One of the issues that came up for discussion with the Board towards the end of 2003 was that of the general dissatisfaction amongst the parents with the services of the dhobis. The parents complained that the washing was poor and clothes were often lost. Why did the school not go in for a modern laundry system? The Board decided, and rightly so, that the services of the dhobis be dispensed with and the school enter into a contract with a laundry service. As the winter vacation was approaching it was felt that this would be a good time to do so. The new term could commence with this new service.

I, for one, had grave doubts about the timing of the whole exercise. The dhobis, I pleaded, had served the school for generations. They ought to be given more time to find an employer who could replace the school. The Board graciously agreed and the dhobis were informed that their services would not be required once the school reopened after the summer vacation in late July.

This was the state of affairs when the union decided to enter the picture. A few months after school reopened in July the leaders of the union sought a meeting with me. How could the school summarily dispense with the services of a group that had served it so loyally for so long? I patiently explained the position of the school on this matter and politely pointed out that since the dhobis were not employees of the school, perhaps the union had no locus-standi in this matter. My explanation carried no weight with the union as they were obviously spoiling for a fight.

Soon the entire support staff was on strike. All services, including catering, came to a grinding halt. I hastily summoned a faculty meeting and spelt out the options. The easiest was to close down the school, which is what the strikers wanted. This would have ensured that we would be at the mercy of the union forever. The cancer would soon spread to all other schools in no time at all. Besides, we had done nothing wrong either legally or morally. The alternative was to keep the school going. This would require a herculean effort in terms of planning, coordination and many, many sleepless hours. The faculty, apart from a few, supported this plan.

What began was virtually a military campaign. The faculty and senior students were divided into groups that alternated duties at different areas and at different times. The idea was that not one day's schedule should be interrupted. We took turns to patrol the campus day and night, to cook food, to clean toilets, to look after the campus and of course to carry on with the business of teaching and learning.

The striking support staff meanwhile became increasingly frustrated. By now local politicians of all hues had jumped in to gain whatever mileage they could. In the midst of all this I took a calculated gamble and suspended the three leaders. This brought other unions into the fray. Hundreds of workers demonstrated outside the campus walls. All the gates were padlocked by the strikers. The leaders staged a 'dharna' outside my residence and loud slogans (including some very abusive ones) were raised. I had a videographer quietly record all this. Press conferences were organized on a daily basis where I met and briefed the press myself. An open invitation was extended to anyone who wished to discuss the matter with me and I was open to suggestions.

At the height of this episode, two politicians representing the two main parties in the state came to visit me. They threatened me with dire consequences if I did not revoke the suspension of the three leaders. I politely informed them that what they were asking for was completely out of the question. In putting up this resistance I drew great strength from the support of my Board and my colleagues. I was in touch with my Chairman on almost an hourly basis and he backed every step that I took. The faculty was marvelous and went way beyond the call of duty in these trying circumstances. The situation outside the walls of the school was getting nastier. A procession was taken out in the town and my effigy burnt at the Clock Tower. This did not bother me as much as the fact that on the same day, at the same venue and time, another group burnt an effigy of a rather dubious politician!

Bricks started being hurled through our windows and suspicious characters armed with sticks started hanging around our gates. Led by some fiery women politicians, forty or fifty wives of the strikers entered my office and harangued me endlessly. Later I was told that these were professional leaders whose services were available for a sum.

At this point I was forced to ask for personal protection and an ex-commando was hired to be my shadow. It was not a pleasant experience and I often wonder how Z category VIPs endure it. The time had come for one of the sides to do something decisive. I decided to move first. I sent out a notice calling for a meeting of the entire staff (teaching and non-teaching) at an appointed hour in the school auditorium. I had the Labour Commissioner in my office when over the telephone the leaders of the strike refused to attend. I filed a complaint of gross indiscipline and insubordination against them as, in addition, the strike had been declared without statutory notice. Consequently, the Labour Commissioner had no hesitation in declaring the strike illegal. Notices were sent out and announcements made declaring that all those interested in continuing to work at the school would have to report for work at eight in the morning the day after failing which their services would be terminated.

In the midst of all this the dhobis had been totally forgotten. In consultation with the Chairman a detailed plan was drawn up. The dhobis (there were eight of them) would be offered alternative employment in the school in any one of the trades available (carpenter, electrician, plumber, driver etc). The school would provide them training in the trade of their choice for a year at the school's cost after which they would be absorbed in the school's roster. It was publicly announced that the dhobis interested in accepting the offer would have to come and sign their appointment orders at an appointed hour and venue.

The Chairman at first baulked at the idea. For a school already overburdened with a huge employee roll this move could prove suicidal. I was, however, supremely confident that the offer would never be accepted. The reasoning behind this belief was that the union would lose its entire raison 'd' etre for the strike. Sure enough, on the appointed day and hour, no one showed up. I had taken the added precaution of having an officer from the Labour Commissioner's office present as witness. The next morning at eight the gates were flung open and all the employees barring the three suspended leaders marched in. The strike was over.

Later that day I called a meeting of the entire staff and assured them that there would be no recrimination. On the contrary, the administration would go out of its way to anticipate the needs of the support staff. Proof that this worked lies in the fact that till the day I relinquished office eight years later there was no union of the support staff in Welham Boys'. Credit must go to my Board, which backed me on every proposal that I made for staff welfare during this period.

When I look back on the events of 2004, I realize had the Board, faculty and students not presented a united front the result would have been quite different. I did not receive any telephone calls of support from other Heads during the crisis. Had we not occupied the legal and moral high ground, the result could have been catastrophic. If the union had been given their way I shudder to think how this flame would have consumed other schools as well. Sadly enough, none of the other schools seemed to realize this at the time, or even later.

26

Boys Will Be Boys?

The support staff were not the only ones who could be recalcitrant. The students and their parents could be equally obtuse. In 2010 I had to deal with a Prefectorial body which had evoked great doubts amongst the faculty about their attitude at the time of their appointment. However, we felt that given the responsibility they would rise to the occasion.

To my great disappointment, one of the first things they did on being appointed was to present me with a list of demands. These were, for the most part, geared to ensure that they would receive more privileges such as frequent outings to town and extra pocket money amongst other things. I sent for the Head Boy, and explained to him that I was deeply disappointed at their attitude. There was not one demand that would benefit the entire student body. I asked him to go back and introspect with his colleagues about what I had said. The next day at breakfast, to my surprise, the Head Boy walked up to me and said that the entire Prefectorial body was resigning. I explained to him that this was not the manner in which I expected this body to conduct itself. If indeed they had genuine grievances, I was quite prepared to listen to them in the presence of other senior faculty after classes gave over at lunch. Subsequently, if they were not satisfied with the proceedings they could resign officially and honourably and be thanked in public for their services. However, the Prefects were adamant. Many of my senior colleagues tried to reason with them but it was water off a duck's back. We even had the respective parents counsel them on the telephone and local guardians summoned to the school, where possible.

This was a distressing situation indeed. Here was a group of boys handpicked by us and vested with the authority to lead the student body and they were being confrontational beyond reason. We were prepared to listen to them and meet them halfway if need be. Yet for reasons unknown they were blocking out all options for a dialogue.

What the boys were doing was tantamount to leading a strike. I was quite sure that if they were allowed to spend the night in their dormitories the entire school would be up in arms the next day. I had a series of telephonic consultations with the Chairman and it was agreed that the Prefects be suspended forthwith. A disciplinary committee meeting was called and an unanimous decision to that effect taken. The parents were duly informed.

Consequently, the parents filed a case against the suspension in the High Court at Nainital. One influential parent even persuaded the anchor of a leading news channel to approach the Chief Minister to move against me. The Chairman, Darshan Singh, very kindly agreed to take on all the legal legwork from his office and we decided to contest the case.

As it happened, Dehradun was hit by the worst part of the monsoon during this period. The roads to Nainital were virtually blocked. The school lawyer felt that an ex-parte decision would be delivered as the lawyer representing the parents was already in situ. Once again, the credibility of the school was at stake. I called for my car and with the school lawyer, the Vice-Principal, Bursar and legal officer, set off for Nainital. The plan was to drive as far as we could and then take a call on how best to manage the rest of the journey. Mercifully we were able to drive all the way but what would ordinarily have taken us about four hours took close to twelve.

To our surprise, at the hearing the judge, owing to certain reasons, decided to recuse himself from the case. We were told that the matter would now be referred to the court of the Chief Justice, who was then away to Kolkata for the pujas. We took the long drive back but we had at least bought ourselves some time as the Chief Justice would be away for a fortnight. To our surprise, we were informed on Friday that that the matter would come up on the following Monday. We had no choice but to make the long and hazardous journey once again on Sunday.

This time the new judge heard both sides out patiently and summoned us to his Chambers during the lunch recess. There he asked me to explain my stand. I explained to him the background of events and pointed out that if we allowed the Prefects to hold the school to ransom we would be putting the entire school at risk for all time to come. The judge agreed. The suspension was approved; the only caveat being that the boys would have to be reintegrated into the mainstream as soon as they had served their suspension. I found myself in full agreement.

To fight a court case (even if one wins it) against one's own students cannot be regarded as the highlight of one's career as an educator. To my mind this was a case where there were no winners. The boys lost precious study time, we were taken away from our main job of looking after the school, the entire school was disturbed and a great deal of bad blood was generated.

This incident threw up important questions of the role of parents during such circumstances. One of the biggest impediments to the progress of our educational system is the lack of cooperation and partnership between parent and school. It is one of our biggest failures to not be able to evolve a culture of partnership between the parents and school. In the old days, parents were quite content to hand over the child to school secure in the belief that the school would do its best for the child. This naivete had its own pitfalls and perhaps led even to some abusive practices being adopted by unethical schools. Now the pendulum seems to have swung to the other extreme particularly with the media, ever anxious for a story, having jumped into the fray. TV channels are quick to pull the trigger and bring in panels of experts to pass judgement on what may have happened in a particular school and the voices of the school Principal or the teachers are completely lost in the din. Too often parents see their role vis-à-vis the school as one of 'them' and 'us'. The truth remains that for educational institutions to be successful a genuine partnership must be forged between the school and the parent in the same way that good parenting involves a partnership between the father and mother. This symbiotic relationship must not be lost in the clamour generated by petty issues. I daresay, both parents and schools need to work very hard to build a partnership and eliminate the trust deficit if education is to be truly meaningful.

Nothing illustrates this better than an incident that took place during my tenure at Welham Boys'. Around Diwali there was an outbreak of one of the dreaded flus (it was either bird or swine, I do not remember clearly) in and around Dehradun and schools were closing down indefinitely. The faculty at Welham and I took the view that given the uncertain nature of the threat, it would be wiser to keep the school going and do everything to ensure that the students were well protected from the disease. We, therefore, decided to disallow our students from going out of the campus, put various health measures in place and restricted the entry of outsiders into the school. Unfortunately, this period of isolation coincided with Diwali and a large number of parents started bombarding me with telephone calls and letters to lift this moratorium. In vain I tried to explain to them that all this was being done to protect their own children. When the calls and letters did not work, pressure was brought on through politicians and bureaucrats. When that tactic did not yield results the media was roped in and local TV channels reported about the supposed brutal dictatorship unleashed in Welham Boys'.

When all failed, a bunch of goons was hired on Diwali day to 'rough me up.' I invited the motley crew into my office and heard their rants about my brutality patiently. Then I asked two randomly chosen students to take the gentlemen on a guided tour of the campus including the dormitories. They saw that we had planned a huge food festival on the day along with a fireworks bonanza by pooling in everyone's fireworks and setting them off under adult supervision. The boys were having a whale of a time. The party meant to 'rough me up' came back to my office, looking very sheepish and apologized profusely.

Another example of this kind of situation was provided by the conflict over false medical certificates. I had been fighting a virtual crusade against the practice of producing false medical certificates in order to secure leave for weddings, birthdays and other such occasions. My plea to the parents was simple, 'When you as a parent tell me that your child is ill, I have no reason to distrust you. Please do not insult our relationship by producing a false certificate.'

The plea, however, fell on deaf ears. One Monday morning I found a bunch of such certificates on my desk. Of the lot, one was from Dehradun, two were from the nearby city of Moradabad and one was from Delhi. Enough is enough, I told myself and set off in my car to investigate. The first stop was the house in Dehradun where the student who had apparently broken his leg over the weekend resided. I found the young man playing cricket with his father on the lawn. I politely asked the father to collect his son's transfer certificate from my office as soon as it was convenient for him. The father became abusive and almost violent. A four hour drive took me to Moradabad to the nursing home from where the certificates had emanated. I asked to see the patients and was told that they had just been discharged. Thereupon, I asked for the medical records. At this point, the doctor who had signed the certificates sheepishly informed me that the boys in question were from the family that owned the nursing home and that he had little choice in the matter. I drove on to the house where the boys lived and as I was denied entry left a message to the parents about collecting their ward's transfer certificates.

A team under the vice-principal was dispatched to Delhi to the well-known hospital from where the last certificate had come. Once again, the records revealed no such patient. I wrote a stern letter to the director of the hospital but received no reply. The boy, however, received his transfer certificate by post.

We just cannot move forward in our educational endeavours unless parents and schools learn to trust each other. A token PTA is not the answer. At Lawrence School I used to encourage the parents to invite teachers home (particularly when they went as escorts on the train journeys during the school vacation). This gave the parents and teachers a chance to get to know each other and the teacher to experience a new place. Our PTA then built on this initiative and started funding one teacher each year to make a trip abroad for professional development.

While it was very dismaying to have to deal with this kind of situation, it was perhaps a bit more dismaying to hear the reaction of the head of one of the better known schools in the country. When I related this incident to him, his reaction was, 'Why get worked up about these things? After all, you cannot change the country!'

That was precisely the point I was making. How can teachers, of all people, give up on this battle? I compare this situation to our soldiers at the border laying down their arms in the face of the enemy. As teachers we have been entrusted with the sacred duty of teaching our children to distinguish between right and wrong. It is tantamount to a sin to fail in this duty.

27

The Heart Rules the Body

All my struggles at Welham Boys' were not of a professional nature. There were some personal ones as well, particularly related to my health. I had taken up the reins of office at Welham in the August of 2003, close on the heels of a condition allied to an infection of the heart. A serious dose of IV antibiotics had helped me through but as I was to discover, the condition had not been cured. Towards November 2003, I started to feel the bouts of chills and shivers come on again which kept getting progressively worse. Blood tests provided no answers. It was decided that I must undergo an echo test. Once conducted the physician declared that the tests were clear. The bouts of shivering, however, kept getting worse. The cardiologist recommended that I get another echo done in Delhi. This time I was to follow a different procedure—

I was to swallow the camera to facilitate a closer view of the heart.

Indrani and I made the journey to Delhi where the doctor entrusted with the test suggested that I do a normal echo before subjecting myself to the painful business of swallowing a camera. The test detected an infective mess much like a ball of hair and quite apparent to the naked eye lodged in my heart. 'Your physician in Dehradun must have been either blind or drunk to miss that,' said the doctor. This, he said, was an emergency. If that ball were to shift for some reason the consequences could be fatal. It would have to be removed surgically through an open heart surgery, one which had to be performed the next morning.

The suddenness of this turn of events shook us. We sat in the hospital reception and debated our next move. This was our first visit to this hospital. While we knew that the doctors were excellent, we had not had an opportunity to establish any relationships here. A quick call was made to our treating physician Dr Ravi Kishore, at Bangalore. He too stressed the need for immediate surgery but felt that if indeed we were more at ease in his care we should take the calculated risk of flying to Bangalore immediately. Indrani immediately rushed back to Dehradun to admit our younger daughter to the boarding arrangement at Welham Girls' where she was studying—a request to which the school kindly agreed.

In the meantime, with a ticket purchased by my brother-in-law, Joy Bhaatacharjya. I flew to Bangalore. Our old friend, Anita Reddy, was there to receive me and drive me straight to the hospital. I was admitted right away to the ICU and the surgery was scheduled for the next morning. While I was being prepared for the surgery one of the young medics on duty cheerfully informed me that the last patient they had with a similar problem died whilst he was being prepared for the operation the evening before.

Armed with that cheerful bit of news, I was wheeled into the operation theatre the next morning. Indrani just about made it to sign the consent papers and then sat outside alone for the next seven hours while the doctors worked on me.

I can hardly bear to think of how those seven hours must have passed for her.

Once the surgery was completed the surgeon assured Indrani that the endevaour had been a success but we would have to wait for another forty-eight hours before we could be sure. This was the most complicated surgery that he had ever attempted, he confessed, adding that he had gone in 'with a scalpel in his hands and a prayer on his lips.'

With the surgery over the pain began. It was relentless, tearing every nerve in my body and it went on unabated. Indrani did the best she could given that time for visitors in the ICU was very limited. After about two weeks I was declared fit enough to be discharged.

After my experience with the management of Heritage School my greatest fear was not of a botched surgery but of losing my job. Darshan Singh was, however, hugely supportive. And so I returned to Welham Boys' in the January of 2004 determined to give the school the best shot that I was capable of. The school was growing from strength to strength as the years passed and my health problems seemed to be a thing of the past. The strike had been sorted out and the future looked promising.

In January 2005 I was invited by the alumni in Mumbai for a fundraising dinner. I was staying at one of the lesser known hotels near Delhi airport before catching the flight early next morning when all of a sudden at night I started feeling very ill. I quickly called the school doctor on the phone and he advised me either to report to a hospital in Delhi or proceed immediately for Dehradun. I decided on the latter option. As the taxi sped through the night on its way to Dehradun I had a grim premonition when I began vomiting blood. Every now and then I had to ask the driver to stop whilst I heaved up bucketfuls of blood. Indrani and the doctor were waiting for me when I pulled up to my residence. I was quickly shifted to my car and driven off to the gastroentologist's nursing home. I was put on a stomach pump. That science can device something capable of causing so much pain is beyond belief. Subjected to about twelve hours of this torture I mercifully sank into oblivion. Little did I know that this was only the beginning. Once home, I started slipping into ventricular tachycardia (a condition where the heart races so fast that one goes into cardiac arrest) and had to be rushed to Delhi. A week or so of treatment there and the doctors seemed confident that they had dealt with the condition successfully.

Alas that was not to be. Once in Dehradun the symptoms started all over again. I seemed to be slipping into a coma. The Dehradun doctors held out no hope. But Indrani would not take 'no' for an answer. She summoned the local ambulance, loaded me in and with the school doctor raced through the night to Delhi. All through the journey the two had to hang on to the IV drip which threatened to get dislodged on account of the bumpy ride.

As it turned out, the situation was much worse than we had thought. Apparently not only the heart but also the liver and kidneys were on the verge of failure. This was a severe reaction to the drugs I was then taking for my heart condition. I soon slipped into a semi-coma. The doctors advised Indrani to assemble the family together. She would have none of it. She accosted Dr Kler, the treating physician, and told him in no uncertain terms that she was fully confident that he would pull me through. Dr Kler told us later that she left him with no choice!

The three odd months that I spent in a semi-coma have become a confused blur in my mind. There are bits and pieces that I remember but it is very difficult to separate the hallucinatory bits from the real ones. I do remember that on our twenty-fifth wedding anniversary that fell in the midst of all this, the nursing staff organized a cake for us. Amidst the hallucinations what does remain real and stamped on my memory is the pain. It was as if every sinew, every nerve in my body was being torn apart. In all my waking moments I would plead with the doctors to let me go.

As for Indrani, I cannot even imagine what she must have gone through. She was consigned to sleeping on a couch outside the ICU for those three months and visiting me for about fifteen minutes at a time, four times a day. Two old students of ours from Lovedale came whenever they could and kept her company. We were overwhelmed with gratitude.

Each time the doctor went past Indrani would ask, 'Is there any improvement?'

To which the doctor would invariably reply, 'None yet.'

Indrani would retort, 'But there is no deterioration either?'

Later I was told that the doctors had christened me, 'The man who refuses to die.' Maybe, 'The husband whose wife does not know how to give up' would have been more appropriate!

The other great sufferers were my daughters. The older one, Diya, was at university in Kolkata and we tried very hard to keep her insulated which made things even more difficult for her. The younger one, Shama, was appearing for her board examinations and we had to leave her alone in the house to fend for herself. To her credit, she never once complained. It was with the support of this marvellous courage displayed by my family that I soldiered on. Indrani would sit by my bed and whisper in my ear, 'This is the last lap before you finish the marathon. The stadium is full of people cheering you on! Go for gold!' Memories of the Barnsley marathon would come flooding back!

Support came from many friends as well. Darshan Singh very graciously extended a handsome loan to me to enable the purchase of an implantable defibrillator which I needed. Support also came from a very unexpected quarter. Dr Kler also happened to be the physician to the Prime Minister, Dr Manmohan Singh. He mentioned my case to Dr Singh and his wife Gurcharan Kaur, who had heard of me from one of her nieces who was a teacher at Welham Boys'. One day, while Indrani was waiting to be allowed into the ICU to visit she was summoned to the hospital office through the PA system. She went with her heart thumping dreading the worst only to find that Mrs Gurcharan Kaur was on the phone for her.

'Don't worry, child,' she said. 'All will be well. We are all praying for you. Have faith.'

It was a wonderfully warm gesture given the circumstances. It did a world of good to both of us. Later we had the opportunity to visit Mrs Kaur at the Prime Minister's residence to thank her, where we were received with great grace and warmth.

Towards the middle of March, by some sheer miracle, I seemed to be improving. The doctors felt confident enough to do something about my condition. It seemed that a very complicated surgery was necessary by which a defibrillator could be implanted in my abdomen and connected to my heart through an abdominal vein as all my major veins had been 'thrombosed' or thickened because of the innumerable surgeries. Such a procedure was apparently very rare in the history of medicine. It is a tribute to the skill of our doctors that they performed this procedure successfully, so much so that till today I have not had a single issue relating to my heart. Later the team that performed this surgery was to contribute an article on their feat to the Indian Heart Journal.

When I visited Dr Kler for my follow up I said, 'Doc, it is really good to see you!'

'Dev,' he replied. 'You have no idea of how good it is to see you alive!'

With that, he promptly had a photograph taken with us to adorn his office wall.

28

An Abrupt End

By the year 2011, the school seemed very secure in its moorings. Welham Boys' seemed to be surging forward in every direction. Not only were the board examination results excellent the students, more importantly, were demonstrating a spirit of enquiry and taking ownership of the learning process. Welham was second to none in sports, neither did it lag behind in co-curricular achievements. Our boys were producing films that won National Awards. Discipline was no longer an issue and Prefects and Housemasters worked in close cohesion. I had even broken a male bastion and appointed the school's first-ever girl Prefect! The morale of both the faculty and the support staff was high and they enjoyed the benefits of a relatively handsome remuneration package. I was very content with the manner in which we were progressing although I was sure that a great deal remained to be done. The upcoming Platinum Jubilee (for which we had already started preparations) scheduled for 2013 seemed to be a befitting milestone. I had been given an extension on my service till 2013 and the Board had told me that after that date it would purely be my call as to whether I wished to carry on or not.

Indrani continued to play a withdrawn if pivotal role in the welfare of the school. Not only was she an excellent teacher and Head of Department, she also pioneered several innovations such as the Model United Nations, the culture of quizzing and the 'Each One Teach One' program, whereby each senior student took on the responsibility of teaching the child of a member of the support staff. Moreover, she continued to combine these duties with those of being a hostess which, as in Lawrence School, were of a fairly demanding nature. Our home continued to be open to faculty, students and school guests and they could be sure that they would be greeted with a smile and refreshments no matter how busy Indrani may have been with other school duties.

As if to reinforce this feel-good factor, the Chairman in the minutes of the Board meeting held on 6th March 2011 at the India International Centre in Delhi, inserted this paragraph:

> 'Item 7: The School passes through various difficulties from time to time. At the same time it is imperative to raise the standards of the school in all areas—Academics, Sports, Team Spirit, Staff Relations, etc. In all these areas the Principal, Mr Dev Lahiri, has played a stellar role and has upheld very well the task that the Board has entrusted to him. In all this he has built a strong team within the school and this has also become a source of strength and future success for the school. Taking note of all these efforts the Board recorded its appreciation of the efforts of Mr Dev Lahiri as Principal of WBS.'

Given this occurrence, imagine my surprise when six Board members (of a total of fourteen) trooped into the office in response to the Chairman's call for an emergency meeting on the 30th of April. There were four local members and the Chairman and representative of the alumni (a nominee of the Chairman) had flown in from Delhi. They went into a huddle and then the Chairman summoned me alone into the adjoining conference room. There he informed me that the entire Board (the rest had apparently been consulted on the phone) was in agreement that I be asked to relinquish my post. When I asked for the reason, Darshan Singh simply announced that my style of management was 'no longer appropriate to the needs of the school.' When I drew his attention to the minutes of the Board meeting which had taken place in March where my style of management had come in for fulsome praise, I was tersely told that was 'history'.

We had had our minor disagreements on the way as any two professionals working very closely on an almost day-to-day basis are bound to have. In fact, heated exchanges also occurred at times. But I had never once imagined that this could lead to a parting of ways particularly because I felt that both of us knew that we had only one end in mind—the welfare of the school. Our differences of opinion were always on issues relating to the school and never personal ones. The school was a huge emotional investment and could easily arouse raw passions in both of us.

Needless to say, this sudden turn of events left me thunderstruck. I had just been granted a three-year extension of my services a few months ago and all my planning had been done accordingly. I still had a huge loan to pay off for my house which had not yet been completed. However, faced with the fact that I had crossed the threshold of sixty years I had several issues to consider. I had precious little in the bank, an unpredictable health problem, a defibrillator to replace every five years at an astronomical cost and two daughters who still looked to me for help. I thus decided that to argue with a line up of powerful people on my own would not be the most prudent thing to do. Besides, it did not make sense to carry on if indeed, as I had been told, the entire Board did not want me to continue.

The last, I discovered, was far from the truth. One of the Board members, Malvika Rajkotia, an eminent Delhi lawyer, resigned in protest and wrote a strong letter to the Chairman, condemning the completely autocratic manner in which this exercise had been conducted. At least four others whom I contacted on the phone said that they had no idea why the Chairman had taken this decision.

One member and his wife actually dropped in when we were packing to leave, to express sorrow and regret that such a thing had happened, and to assure us that whilst this particular member had been present at the meeting, he had not been party to the decision.

It goes without saying that Indrani and I have spent agonizing hours wondering about the reason for this sudden decision of the Chairman (and by all accounts it was completely his decision alone) to part company with us. The three main reasons why a head of organization can be asked to go are incompetence, financial irregularities and moral turpitude. The first could not obviously apply to me as the Board had recently recorded a minute praising my leadership. It could not be the second as they had not thought it fit to bring any charges against me. In fact, the Chairman had publicly declared that my integrity was beyond doubt. As for the third, once again no mention of moral turpitude had been made leave alone any formal charge. Surely, if there was any reason for official displeasure I should have been summoned by the Board and told about it. Till this day we are searching for the answer.

All my attempts to find out from the Board the reasoning behind the decision was met with silence. On 3rd June 2011, I had written to the Board:

Dev Lahiri
"Jannat"
P.O. Ganghora
Ganghol Panditwari
Dehradun

3rd June, 2011

The Chairman, Board of Governors
Welham Boys School,
Dehra Dun.

Dear Sir,

I have been wondering for a long time whether or not I should send you this mail as previous attempts to communicate with you seem to have failed. However, the fact remains that we worked together as a team for the better part of eight years and saw some good and some bad times through together. So I did feel that I owed you this letter.

To begin with I must confess that both of us are still in a state of utter shock after the 30th of April. We had met officially on the 6th March in Delhi and subsequently unofficially for lunch at my house when my friend Sally was present. On neither occasion did I get the impression that you were upset with me. At any rate, I was always under the impression that if you ever had something on your mind you would confront me directly with it. After all we have worked together on almost a day to day basis for so long. And I can say with complete conviction that whilst I may have had my faults and made my mistakes I served the school loyally, honestly and to the best of my ability. I, therefore feel that if you had been told anything about me you ought to have summoned me directly and demanded an explanation - as indeed was your right as Chairman. If I could not have supplied a satisfactory explanation you had every right, as well to take the call of your choice. As things happened, I cannot help but feel that I was denied this elementary privilege. Sir, you entrusted me with the lives of over five hundred children. Surely you could have heard me out directly? I have shown nothing but the highest regard and respect for you during our entire association. Perhaps I deserved a hearing at least?

As things stand all that is so much water under the bridge now. All I am asking is that we get a generous & honourable settlement that includes a respectable pension, perhaps an opportunity to meet either with you or the full Board so as to understand where we went wrong and an opportunity to explain my position so that the air is cleared, and finally an honorable exit so that we can visit the school we served for so long with our heads held high instead of having to slink off like some criminals. Surely these are not unreasonable demands given the length and quality of our service, and what we have achieved with the school in the last eight years?

I look forward to a sympathetic consideration of our request.

Regards,

Warm regards

Yours sincerely,

Dev Lahiri

Cc: All Board members

Till this day the Board has maintained a studied silence. At the end of it we were left wondering that if this was the state of affairs in one of the country's better known schools what might be transpiring in the 'lesser' institutions?'

What was as mystifying as the Board's decision to part company with us was their decision to block us out of the school completely. Almost as soon as we reached home after the meeting we found the gate connecting our residence to the school heavily padlocked and guarded by security personnel. This was to keep the staff and students from visiting us. The faculty's request to see us off with a farewell gathering was firmly refused. The Board, at the time of my resignation, had assured me that they would look sympathetically at my request for a pension. Indeed that intention had been minuted at a previous Board meeting. Now I was told in no uncertain terms that a pension was out of the question.

And it did not end there. Some months later, much after we had vacated our official residence and moved out of campus, I was involved in a very serious accident that occurred, coincidentally, right next to the school. As I was bleeding profusely and in a state of shock Indrani rushed me for medical attention to the closest possible source of help which, as it happened, was Welham Boys'. To our horror the guard at the gate politely folded his hands and begged us not to embarrass him as he had strict orders not to let us enter. Our bewilderment at this attitude was heightened by the fact that the Board had on it at least one serving and some retired Heads of schools in addition to a retired army officer of the rank of a Lieutenant General. Surely they would know better about tradition and protocol with respect to the ex-Head of an institution?

A year later, we had a chance to clear the mystery when we were on our way to take up an assignment in the U.S.A. One of the Governors of Welham Boys' (the alumni representative), much to our surprise, invited us for coffee on the day we were to fly out. During the course of our conversation I naturally enough asked him if he knew why we had been asked to leave the service of the school. He had no answer except that it was the Chairman's will. I then asked him why we were being kept out of the campus with such a sense of vengeance.

His answer was, 'Sir, do you realize that one speech from you could turn the entire school against the Board?'

I walked away from that conversation overcome with a sense of sadness. To think that the lives of so many young people were being entrusted to a Board that had so little confidence or belief in the validity of its own decision was a frightening thought indeed.

My experiences with the Boards at both Lawrence School and Welham Boys' have made me reflect a great deal on the roles that Boards often play in such schools. In both cases, I had Boards that apart from meeting at prescribed intervals (and here too, attendance was very sporadic. In the case of Welham Boys' some members did not attend for years) knew very little about what was happening in the school, and contributed even less. Mr M. K. Kaw, the Chairman of the Board of Lawrence School, did not visit the school once during my tenure, which was not surprising, considering how huge his brief was as Secretary, Education, Govt of India.

At Welham, the only Board member who took any interest in the school was the Chairman, Darshan Singh. This, in addition to the fact that he was Chairman for life, was probably the reason why something of this nature could occur at all.

Yet these were the people entrusted with making decisions that impacted the lives of young people. What was frightening was the total lack of accountability they enjoyed. When parents, for instance, wrote to the Board at Lawrence about their feelings regarding my stewardship of the school they were ignored. In the case of Welham they were told that I had resigned on grounds of poor health.

What I have also learned is that whilst Boards can do what they wish they cannot sully the relationship between a teacher and his or her students. As with Lovedale, Indrani and I continue to enjoy an extremely close and caring relationship with our old students at Welham. As a matter of fact, almost a year after I left Welham, I was visiting the bank that services the school (and is located right next to it) when word got out to the campus that I was on the bank premises. A large number of students and faculty came across to meet me and one of them was the school sports captain. He was carrying a crest of the school with him and informed me that he was there on behalf of the entire student body to give me the crest as a farewell gift, as they (the students) had not been given an opportunity to bid us farewell officially.

I took the young man aside and explained to him that while I was really touched by the gesture it would not be appropriate for me to accept any gift which was not given with the blessings of and indeed in the presence of the current head of the school. The young man was not at that point entirely convinced. I hope that some day he will see the sense in what I said.

I have also often wondered along the lines of the 'what if' theory of history. What if I had not taken on the forces working against Lawrence and Welham? What if I had been content to just keep the system going and doing only what was politically correct?

Judging from what I see around me I probably would have had a very safe passage through both places and been spared the trauma that my family and I had to go through. But would it have been fair to the institution? And equally importantly, could I have lived with myself? These are the hard choices life often throws up. In the end a man must do what a man must do. Was I bitter about the incidents that had taken place? Fortunately, the answer was provided by Nelson Mandela when he wrote,

'As I walked out of the door towards the gate that would lead to my freedom, I knew if I did not leave my bitterness and hatred behind, I would still be in that prison.'

For my part, I take great solace in the inscription painted on a beautiful tile which some of my colleagues gifted to me when I was leaving Lawrence School. It reads:

'To our mentor, you let us explore the sky and taught us that the sky is the limit if you dare!'

Many years after I had left Lawrence School and was applying for various positions, I asked a former parent of Lawrence to provide me with a reference. This is what he wrote:

R. Gopalakrishnan
Executive Director

TO WHOM IT MAY CONCERN

I write this note about Dev Lahiri, who was Headmaster of Lawrence School, Lovedale, where all my three children studied. It is not a testimonial, it is an acknowledgement by a parent of contribution by a teacher; it is a tribute to a Headmaster who made a difference, not only to my children, but to all those who passed through the school at that time.

When I worked in Hindustan Lever, Dev Lahiri joined as an idealistic young man in the Communications Department. His stint was brief because neither commerce nor HLL were made for Dev Lahiri. He was a passionate teacher, who wanted to make a difference to education – somehow, he had strayed into the world of business, mercifully for a short time!

In the early 90s, I saw him as Headmaster of Lawrence School, Lovedale. This school had a well-established reputation, built over 125 years, so what could a Headmaster with a limited tenure do for it? A lot, and I witnessed it first hand during the period 1993-1998, when my three children studied there.

Dev Lahiri has passions when it comes to education, and these passions consume him (as passions should!). A passion to inculcate high aspirations, a passion for discipline and camaraderie, a passion for students to not only attain academic excellence but to develop broader interests – in short, a passion to make a difference. Like coins, passions too have their flip side. Dev Lahiri cannot co-exist with mediocrity, he is impatient with people who are obsessed only with marks to the exclusion of other interests. He is committed to professionalism in education and wants his professionalism to be accepted just as a doctor or an engineer would.

As a parent, I preferred a Headmaster who stood for something specific, not a middle-of-the-road, wishy washy Headmaster. And I found that in Dev Lahiri. He is what he is. A huge asset if you share his passions, and can live with the flip side of his passions. I am convinced that Dev Lahiri is destined to make a difference wherever he is because that is his nature, it is his calling in life.

R. Gopalakrishnan

Mumbai
7th May 2003

This is probably how I would like to be remembered as a Head of school.

29

The Wasatch Epilogue

CONTACT BETWEEN the Welham Boys' School and the Wasatch Academy, Utah, an exclusive private boarding school in the U.S.A., began when the telephone rang in my office at Welham one morning in March 2009. A parent of an ex-student of the school requested a meeting for me with the head of Wasatch and their consultant, Dr Chakravarti, an eminent academic based in the U.S.A., both of whom were visiting Indian schools in the quest for a partnership.

Joseph Loftin, the head of Wasatch, turned out to be an extremely unusual man. He had rescued this little school founded in 1875 in the heart of Central Utah from oblivion and in the last twenty years or so as its head made it into one of the leading private boarding schools in the mid-west. The school remarkably hosted students from as many as thirty-eight different nationalities!

As we spoke, Joe and I discovered huge similarities in our visions for education. Joe also had a deep and abiding love for India. As he was staying for a few days Joe attended one of my assemblies at Welham. As soon as we walked out of the hall, Joe said, 'I must have you as the keynote speaker for my school's Graduation Day in May.'

Thus it was that in May I found myself on a plane to Salt

Lake City from where the school was about a hundred miles away. It was a stark but breathtakingly beautiful environment that the school was located in. My speech at the Graduation day obviously went down very well as I found myself surrounded by parents, faculty and students complimenting me on what I had said. Joe, in fact, wrote to my Board (and I quote):

> 'Last weekend Wasatch Academy, Utah's oldest preparatory school, founded in 1875, had the honour of receiving one of the most profound graduation addresses given in the school's long and illustrious history... This year's graduation was my twenty-second as President of Wasatch. In the course of that time our school has had senators, astronauts, highly awarded authors, world renowned scientists, international dignitaries and leading educators address the graduating classes of Wasatch students. Never though have I seen a speaker impact an audience at this event as powerfully as Mr Lahiri... It is an honour that I can consider Dev Lahiri a colleague in this most noble profession. Congratulations to you as trustees of Welham Boys' School for selecting an outstanding leader to serve as your Principal.'

Thus began an extremely fruitful relationship between the two schools. Groups of students from Wasatch visited Welham Boys' and participated together in various projects. Indeed, when the village of Sumgarh was devastated by a flash flood and the school building collapsed killing eighteen children, students from Welham Boys' and Wasatch worked together to start the reconstruction process. Some of our basketball players benefitted immensely from their stint at Wasatch, which boasted of the finest school basketball team in the state of Utah.

When I was trying to cope with the aftershock of the Welham episode, I received a call from Joe inviting Indrani and me to work with him at Wasatch. This was quite unbelievable. In all my years in the profession I had never heard of any Head from India leave alone a retired one being actually invited to work in the U.S.A.!

This was no ordinary invitation either. Joe flew the two of us across in December 2011 for a preliminary visit so that Indrani would have an opportunity to see Wasatch. Then in April 2012, while we were waiting for our visas to come through, we were invited to spend six weeks at the school to familiarise ourselves with the working environment there. Finally when our visas came through in September we joined the faculty.

The Wasatch experience was truly a memorable one. Thrust into a culture that was so different in terms of its educational system, its social and cultural norms, coping was not easy. What really helped, however, was the wonderful warmth and friendship of faculty, staff and students.

I will never forget my first experience with an American teenager on a disciplinary issue. The student had been a repeat offender on various counts and I was asked to deal with him. I asked him to see me in my office the following morning. When I walked into my office the next day I saw a pair of feet sticking up at one end of the sofa in my room and a face covered with a baseball cap at the other end. As I sat in my chair and coughed politely, a hand emerged, lifted the cap and a cheerful voice asked, 'Hey dude, how ya doin?'

I nearly choked...

Indrani, for her part, had her plate full as a Social Sciences teacher. Quite apart from coming to grips with the technology, (it was a 'paperless' school) dealing with students from so many different backgrounds and of such varying abilities, had its own challenges. However, it had its hugely fulfilling moments as well. Indrani pioneered the introduction of the Model United Nations in the school and soon this became not only a very popular activity but one in which the school soon began to excel. As a matter of fact a student wrote about her, 'This is a teacher who expects absolutely the most out of you. She is an incredible woman who is an amazing role model...'

Yet another wrote, 'Mrs Lahiri is one of the most knowledgeable and intuitive persons I have ever met. Not only is she a demanding teacher she is one of the most compassionate and gracious individuals you will ever come across.'

In a society where receiving praise from a teenager is like getting blood out of stone, this was a remarkable achievement indeed!

The faculty were very helpful and friendly and we developed some great friendships, aided of course by some of Indrani's Indian food, which soon became a rage on campus. As I was put in charge of the equestrian program as well I had the unique opportunity to develop some great friendships with genuine cowboys. For someone brought up on a diet of Westerns this was a heaven-sent opportunity.

Wasatch, with its thirty eight nationalities, is truly an amazing experiment in internationalism and both of us felt that schools such as this could truly help make the world a better place. I was given the wonderful opportunity to bring a group of students and some faculty to India and we went right into the country's heartland (the villages of Madhya Pradesh). It was truly heartwarming to see American teenagers interact with our village children and I am quite convinced that for some of them life will not quite be the same again.

One incident that occurred as a fallout of this trip will remain forever etched in my memory. One of the young men whom I had persuaded to come along on the trip was a student who suffered from an 'addiction' to video games and had, as a matter of fact, been sent to 'rehab' for this problem. I persuaded his parents to let him come along on the trip as I was convinced that it could only do him good. One of the ground rules of this trip was that it was 'technology free, implying no cell phones, video games or ipads. Also I was quite sure that an exposure to a culture where such a large number of people lived without devices (we were travelling mainly in the hinterland of Madhya Pradesh in the heart of tiger country, as the main purpose of the trip was to understand the tiger which, incidentally was the mascot of the school), would be an eye-opener.

Of course I was worried that the young man in question might suffer from 'withdrawal symptoms' at being so dramatically removed from his comfort zone. But my fears proved to be completely unfounded. The gentleman was the first to be on time for the early morning safaris. He loved interacting with the village children and he had the most number of questions about all that he saw around him.

Imagine my distress, therefore, when two days after we returned to school in the U.S., I was informed that my young 'advisee' (he was part of a group of students allocated to me for direct supervision) was 'missing'. My colleague, the Dean of Students, and I had a hunch where we might find him. And sure enough, there he was, in the basement toilet of one of the buildings, hunched over his video game.

'What on earth has got into you?' I asked, 'You were so "normal" in India!'

'Mr Lahiri,' replied the young man, 'India was so different. There was so much colour, so much noise, so much to look at. This place is so boring!'

Incredible India indeed!

Wasatch also provided us, as educators, an opportunity to gain some understanding of the educational system in the U.S. and to draw some lessons for India in the process. We learnt from the freedom schools enjoy in planning their own curriculum and awarding their own diplomas. Whilst this has its pitfalls as there is very little uniformity of standards, it certainly is a welcome change from being under the shackles of a monolith like our Boards. As colleges in the U.S. have their own entrance procedures it all levels out at that stage. It gives schools the freedom to develop curricula in accordance with their own philosophy.

Most importantly we found that regardless of the difference in curricula between schools, the movement is away from content to skills. Schools use content more as a vehicle for developing skills that will be essential in the new world order. Skills such as creativity, problem-solving, familiarity with technology, leadership and being a team player. The underlying assumption is that content in this day and age can be accessed anyway. It is only a click away. It is how that content is applied that is more the job of educators.

While it is true that in the U.S., the school education system has swung too far away from content leaving most Americans rather ill-informed about the world around them, in India we have become completely bogged down with content. The syllabus is king and teachers spend all their time and energy in fighting the battle to deliver it. I am afraid that in the process creativity, problem solving, research and reference, all fall by the wayside. The sad truth is that most parents in India send their children not so much to receive an education as to clear a Board examination and secure entry to a college of repute. Somehow, we must arrive at a more equitable balance between 'skills' and 'content'. We must learn to value an education for the sake of an education.

Towards the beginning of our second year there I was unfortunately diagnosed with prostate cancer which would eventually lead to yet another extremely painful surgery. I knew feeling sorry for myself would provide no solutions. At that stage we were also beginning to feel homesick and missing our daughters very much. Given this new challenge, we decided to make tracks for home.

Wasatch does not really have a culture of farewells for its faculty and so were quite amazed at what they did for us. Two special assemblies were organized, one for Indrani and one for me. Indrani was described as being one of the most 'awesome' teachers at Wasatch, though she 'kicked butt'! On the day before we left about sixty students got together and organized a pizza party for us. Given the pivotal role played by the pizza in American culture, this was perhaps the ultimate accolade.

In May 2014, Joe suddenly called and invited us to the graduation ceremony, all expenses paid. We returned to a rousing reception. The warmth and conviviality overwhelmed us. Many of the students that we were very close to were graduating and for them and for us this was quite special.

We have returned from Wasatch hugely enriched and with some special memories. The Dean of Studies wrote just before we left:

> 'We have been fortunate to have hosted you and benefitted from your fine examples and years of quality experience in education and your global perspective. It has been a magical time for us and we are going to miss you. I cannot imagine seeing you replaced but of course we will try. The long and public process of us all saying goodbye is a testimony to the depth of our appreciation.'

A student on scholarship from Mali wrote:

> 'Dear my Parents, (sic) Mr Lahiri and Mrs Lahiri, I am feeling very strong emotions! Since I came to America I have never met people like you guys. I am lucky that I have the privilege of being your son, friend and student.'

A Russian student wrote: 'Thank you for being the mentor that we teenagers of the world today so desperately need. You provide a milestone that I may only hope to reach.'

As any teacher will testify, nothing can give more joy and satisfaction than the love and accolades of one's students. Indrani and I are blessed in that we have had those in plenty.

And we are doubly blessed in the wonderful friendships that we have developed over the years and across the globe at that. Many ask me if the trials and tribulations that I have suffered both professionally and personally have embittered us in any way. If life (and near death) has taught us one thing, it is that there is no time for regret or recrimination. One must move on.

In the immortal words of Scarlett O'Hara in 'Gone with the Wind', 'Tomorrow is another day.'